THEY SPEAK WITH ONE VOICE SERIES 2

THE BIBLE AND EGYPT'S THIRD INTERMEDIATE PERIOD

A CORRELATION OF THE BIBLE AND ARCHAEOLOGY

DR JOHN OSGOOD

Ark House Press
arkhousepress.com

Cataloguing in Publication Data:
Title: The Bible and Egypt's Third Intermediate Period
ISBN: 978-1-7644430-8-1 (pbk)
Subjects: REL006660 (Biblical Studies / History & Culture); REL006220 (Christian Theology / Apologetics); REL006700 (Biblical Archaeology).

Design by initiateagency.com

THE THIRD INTERMEDIATE PERIOD – A REVISED CHRONOLOGY.

A PERIOD OF FRAGMENTATION

CONTENTS

PART 1

INTRODUCTION AND 25th DYNASTY

ABSTRACT

This discussion presents a revised chronology and history of the period known as the "Third Intermediate Period".

It will be argued that the period began during the latter part of the reign of Ramses II, who is here placed in the 8th Century BC, and that, in his later years some event effected his reign. Perhaps a disability, and that the kingdom became fragmented into several contemporary kingdoms, as claimed by Herodotus in a rather garbled account, even while the great king was still alive.

The period was interrupted with the attack of Piye (Piankhi) of Sudan, installing the 25th Dynasty. It ended with the conquest by Assyrian Assurbanipal 664 BC, and the total length of the period then was less than 150 years, not the 500 years presently claimed, by sequential addition of the reigns.

It will be claimed that 21st and 22nd Dynasties and 25th, were significantly contemporary. Additionally, that the 20th Dynasty and the END part of 19th Dynasty which is presently placed following Merenptah, were set up as regional offshoots in Heliopolis and Thebes respectably, while Ramses II was still alive.

It will also be claimed that the Sea People attacked Ramses III (8th year), circa. 755 BC, and that this attack preceded the attack from the west, in Merenptah's 5th year, the latter corresponding in time with Shalmaneser V 's decimation of Northern Israel as indicated in the Merenptah "Israel Stele" 722 BC.

Such a revision brings greater clarity to the correlation of the Bible and archaeology during the period of the Kings.

The presentation will be divided into several parts to aid assimilation of the huge subject matter that is the "Third Intermediate period"

KEYWORDS

Ramses II, 25th Dynasty, 22nd Dynasty, 21st Dynasty, 20th Dynasty, Sea People, 24th Dynasty.

INTRODUCTION

The period here under discussion is usually known as the Third Intermediate Period, and in conventional terms would occupy 1186 - 664 BC (Manley, 1996), a period of over 500 years. This is from the standard sequential interpretation by the modern authors of the arrangement of the dynasties from the end of the 19th until the beginning of the 26th dynasties.

There is, however, good reason to believe that this period was of the order of less than 150 years, a claim that will instantly be dismissed by some, but this discussion will attempt to uphold that claim.

I believe the key to this can be found in a garbled account by Herodotus (Book 2)

> *"After the reign of Sethos—Unable, however, to do without a king for long, they divided Egypt into twelve regions and appointed a king for each of them. United by intermarriage, the twelve kings governed in mutual friendliness on the understanding that none of them should attempt to oust any of the others, or to increase his power at the expense of the rest."*

Such is, of course, an extraordinary statement for such a realm as Egypt, but should not be dismissed without genuine consideration.

The following are the implications:-

1) The 'Sethos' here is almost certainly Seti 1 of the 19th Dynasty, who was a significant military figure. So, the period indicated would fall after his reign.
2) A period of either no king, which is unlikely, or the impotence of the reigning king, an alternate meaning to *"Unable, however, to do without a king"*
3) A regionalisation of Egypt.
4) Parallel dynasties.
5) Significant intermarriage.
6) A degree of mutual co-operation.

Now despite the garbled account, there is almost certainly a kernel of truth here, for when Kushite king Piye (Dyn. 25) conquered Egypt he found a possible 20 kings. Then a small time after this, when Assyrian Assurbanipal conquered Egypt, in 664 BC, he also found around 20 kings. There was clearly regionalisation.

SOME AUTHORITIES ALREADY RECOGNISE A PROBLEM WITH CONVENTIONAL INTERPRETATION

Pertinent here are 3 quotes from Egyptologists which recognise a politically chaotic period, during the time recognised as the "third Intermediate Period".

> *James, Peter 2013, p. 243.*
>
> *"—And there is nothing untoward about three year-counts during the politically fragmented Egypt of the Third Intermediate period, with its rival kings and somewhat awkward power-sharing arrangements."*

> *Aston, David, 2014. ch 2, p.16*
>
> *"—Recent studies have shown that it is becoming increasingly clear that during the reign of Orsorkon II, the Egyptian kingship was being split into a more feudal society, or a loose confederation reinforced by family alliances and appointments, in which several kings were reigning at the same time, many of whom were clearly not known to the compilers of the records consulted by Manetho."*
>
> *Ad Thijs, 2011, p163-181.*
>
> *"The concept of the 20th Dynasty as a monolithic block began to crumble when the evidence from the tomb-robbery papyri forced us to accept a split during the reign of Ramses IX. Our working hypothesis for the Banishment Stele would simply add a third Royal House alongside the two Ramesside lines already known.*
>
> *There is no a priori reason why during this phase of Egyptian history the country could not already have been broken up into more separate kingdoms than the two established so far. Instead of treating this possibility as anathema, which would be a dogmatic stance, we will here take a more open approach and simply take the Banishment Stele as a serious indication that the disintegration of Egypt may well have set in a few years earlier than hitherto assumed."*

Now the king who followed Seti I was Ramses II, and to some this would clearly rule out what Herodotus is claiming. However, a close examination of this period suggests that the real military genius of the dynasty was Seti I, and Ramses fell short of his father's achievements, and was, rather, the great propagandist, and clearly highly successful in that capacity.

The long reign of Ramses II has much to inform us in the early days of that reign, but as Petrie states (Sir Flinders Petrie, -History of Egypt III, p.71):-

> *Of the latter part of the reign there are no records, except a few trivial papyri and ostraka."*

Not a huge amount has changed since that was written, and he continues . p.72:-

> *'it seems then that a long period of gradual decline occupied the greater part of this much boasted reign."*

This would have occupied around 30 years, and in fact the decline must have constituted an incapacity, because this appears to be a signal for the securing of territories by multiple dynasties, as I will continue to show, and that, while the great king was still alive. This is one of the conditions for Herotodus' claim, an incapacitated king, and that following soon after the reign of Seti1 (Sethos).

As discussion of the various dynasties proceeds, I will eventually point out that events of the later period of Ramses II in fact set in train the happenings of the 'Third Intermediate Period'.

I will discuss the mechanism of this fragmentation, but certain basics of this revision need to be stated.

1) The reign of Ramses II is here held to be 792-727 BC, and this is consequent on accepting Merenptah's statement in his 5th year - *"Israel is laid waste - its seed is no more"*, to be a reference to the Assyrian ending of the northern kingdom of Israel, and not a reference to any conquest by Merenptah (Courville). The now aged Merenptah had just been defending a Libyan attack from the west by the Sea People, at the same time as the Assyrian Shalmaneser V was attacking Palestine and especially Egypt's faithful vassal Northern Israel. That kingdom had been a faithful vassal ever since the days of Jeroboam I, and the Bible does not indicate any 'hostile' attack by Egyptian armies on Northern Israel (likely military assistance) despite the attacks on Judah, the north's antagonist. The details of that relationship will reveal themselves during the discussion.
2) Here I believe David Rohl (A Test of Time) has convincingly shown that the 21st and 22nd Dynasties were largely contemporary.
3) When it comes to the political negotiation of claims to territory, those territories already held become potent bargaining chips, and it was politic to

install members of one's own family over as many cities as able, and such would explain why this period saw so many co-regencies, and contemporary kings, as will be outlined.

THE PLACE OF THE 25TH DYNASTY

One of the stabilizers of the chronology of this period is the attack by Kushite Piye (Piankhi) on Egypt and the establishment of the 25th Dynasty. For kings of this period find their reference in both the Bible and the Egyptian records. The dates given by different authors have been manifold. The following is how I see the situation.

In JEA 79, 1993, Leo Depuydt (p. 269) wrote:-

> *"With 690 BC, the explorers of Egyptian chronology have reached the edge of familiar territory on their journey into the past and are overlooking a vast unmapped area into which it is possible to make expeditions, but of which no precise measurements can be obtained—."*

(690 BC is the date of Taharqa's accession)

Such is the state of Egyptian chronology, which is held up as the yardstick of the ancient world, and against which the more sure Biblical Chronology is often downgraded.

In the same article he attempts to obtain the details of the 25th Dynasty, particularly the date of Piye's invasion.- he arrives at the date 709 BC.

In the same year, Alberto R. Green (1993) concludes that the date of the invasion was 727 BC

However, on perusing the Assyrian records (Luckenbill, ARAB 2- 62 and 79), we find that Sargon II (721-706 BC), states- *"—to the border of Egypt which is on the frontier of Meluhha (Ethiopia)"*

Indicating that at that moment (towards the later years of Sargon's reign) Egypt was still independent of the Kushite Kingdom. But then Sennacherib (705-681

BC) in his third campaign, 701 BC, clashes with a combined force of Egyptian and Ethiopian troops (ARAB 2-240).

The point is that the invasion of Egypt by Piye sits more comfortably just before Sennacherib's campaign, but after the statement earlier made by Sargon, who came to power 722 / 21 BC.

DePuydt appears to choose the Minimal Chronology as follows:-

Piye	728-706 BC (Egyptian campaign - 709 BC- his 20th year)
Shabaka	706-692 BC (invades Egypt 705 BC)
Shabataka (Shebitko)	(692-690 BC)
Taharqa	690-664 BC

Depuydt, however reasons that any new found year dates could make the invasion a couple of years earlier.

Recent findings, however, have led to the claim that Kushite Shabataka (Shebitko) preceded Shabaka on the throne, as a result of the reading of the Tang-i-var inscription of Sargon, which indicates that Shebitko was the king who returned the rebel Iamani to Sargon, and that would be 707 BC.

Now as we know that Piye's latest known year date was year 24, this then adds at least 4 more years to 707 BC, which then makes the invasion of Piye 711 BC. This is the date we will use here.

PIYE'S CAMPAIGN INTO EGYPT IS HERE HELD TO BE 711 BC -A FOUNDATION DATE!!

We will then date these kings:-

Piye	730-708 BC
Shebitko	707- 705 BC execution of Bakenranef (24th Dyn.) 705 BC
Shabaka	704 - 691 BC
Taharqa	690 - 664 BC

Conquest by Assurbanipal and termination of "Third Intermediate Period" -664 BC

We then, also have a genealogy of the Kushite Dynasty as follows:-

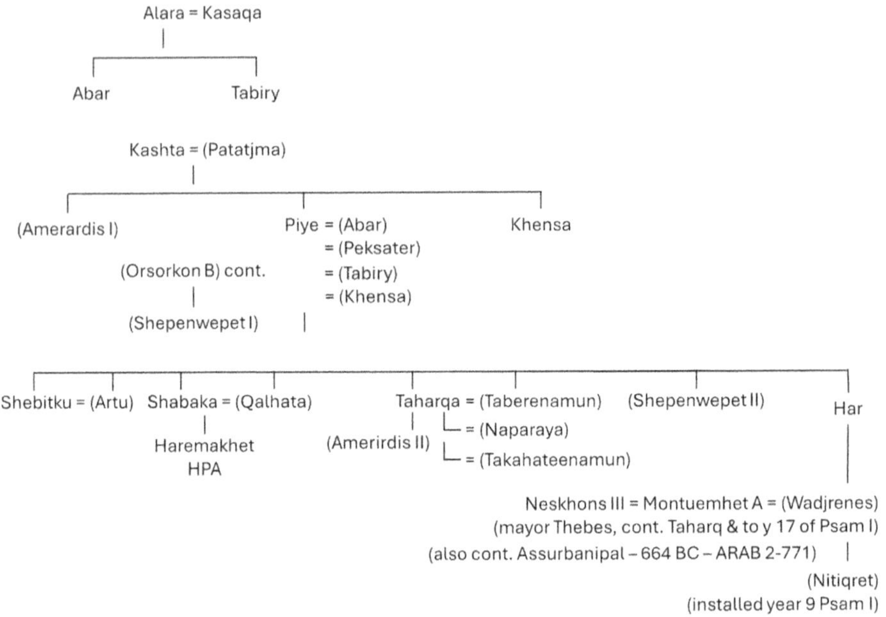

(some small variations have been advanced by different authors - e.g some consider Shabaka to be a brother of Piye, however such does not affect materially the discussion here)

CONQUEST OF PIYE (earlier called Piankhi) - THE PIANKHI STELE

When Piye invaded then in 711BC, he named the following kings (I have added appropriate identifications consistent with the present discussion)

Nimlot over Hermopolis - almost certainly NIMLOT D, son of Takelot II, over Hermopolis (in association with Peftjauawybast over Heracleopolis)

SHESHONK chief of the Ma in Busiris. - Sheshonk III

Yewepet = IUPUT over Leontopolis, almost certainly IUPUT 1 (& II see later) son of Pedubast 1

ORSORKON in per Bast (Bubastis), almost certainly an aged (possibly almost near terminal) Orsorkon II in Bubastis (and Tanis) - the Silkanni of Sargon.

Bakaneffi = Bakeneffi A son of Sheshonk III at Arthribis.

PEFTJAUAWYBAST in Heracleopolis (magna), son-in-law to Rudamun.

Pediese (A) father of Peftauawybast, hereditary prince, High Priest (HPM) Memphis

TEFNAKHT 1 (Wahibre, Iribre, see later under 24th Dynasty)

As well as a number of other kings especially from the western delta.

SHESHONK chief of the Ma at Busiris, is almost certainly Sheshonk III, but there is no evidence that Piye went as far north as Tanis. But as the discussion proceeds, it seems that Piye's invasion equates more easily with the time of Sheshonk III than Sheshonk V as presently commonly held, which is also illustrated by Bierbrier chart XIIIA - D p. 56-59 (Peftauawybast). This is an important, and in fact pivotal point, and failure here is the cause of much confusion with the conventional chronology.

PIYE'S CONQUEST WAS DURING THE REIGN OF SHESHONK III

Readers will recognise that the above identifications are not the usual ones, but I will justify them as we proceed, for I believe that the conquest of Piye has been correlated too late in the 22nd Dynasty, and should be placed earlier. As a result, incorrect assumptions have been made.

CERTAIN PRE-EMPTIVE CONCLUSIONS WILL BE MADE -relevant to Dyn. 25

1) The 25th Dynasty began within a couple of years of the termination of the 19th Dynasty.
2) The 25th Dynasty ran alongside and over the latter part of the 22nd Dynasty, rather than ending it.
3) A case will be made in part 2, that Piye's invasion 711 BC corresponds closely with year 30 of Sheshonk III - (Apis stele Sheshonk III).
4) Sheshonk III will be identified as "king So" of 2 Kings 17:4, to whom Hoshea appealed, likely in Shalmaneser's 2nd year -circa. 726 BC, Sheshonk's 15th year. The Semitic / Assyrian rendering of 'Sheshonk' is (SO)sinki or (SU) sinku (ARAB 2-771).Shebitko followed Piye on the throne and delivered his captive to Sargon in 707 BC.
5) Shabako followed Shebitko and clashed unsuccessfully at Eltekeh in Palestine with Sennacherib during Sennacheb's first campaign against Hezekiah - 701 BC.
6) On Sennacherib's second and fateful campaign against Hezekiah 689 BC, Tarharqa (Dyn. 25) mobilised to defend Judah but turned back without conflict, Isaiah 37:9.

REFERENCES

Aston, David 2014, "Royal Burials of Thebes during the first Millennium BC' Ch 2 p 16 of- "Thebes in the First Millennium BC', Cambridge Scholars Publishing, edited by Elena Pischikova, Julia Budka,and Kenneth Griffin.

Bierbrier, M.L. 1975, The late New Kingdom in Egypt, Aris & Philips Ltd Warminster.

Courville, Donovan, The Exodus problem and its Ramifications, vol 1, Loma Linda.

Depuydt Leo, Journal of Egyptian Archaeology 19, 1993, p 269.

Green, Alberto R.W. 1993, Journal of Near Eastern Studies, 52, no. 2, The identity of King So of Egypt.

Herodotus The Histories Book 2, p.154,124, Penguin Classics. 1954 Great Britain

James, Peter 2013, Two Studies in 21st Dynasty History 1: Deconstructing Manetho's 21st Dynasty II: The dateline of High Priest Menkheperre. Journal of Egyptian Archaeology 6:1 P.219-256.

Luckenbill ARAB 2 Ancient Records of Assyria and Babylonia, vol. 2, section 62 and 79. 1927, University of Chicago Press

Manley, Bill, 1996. The Penguin Historical Atlas of Ancient Egypt. p. 134-5.

Petrie, Sir Flinders, The History of Egypt vol III. p 71. 1905, Methuen & co. London.

Rohl, David, A Test of Time, 1995, Century Publications.

Thijs, Ad 2011, Introducing the Banishment Stele into the 20th Dynasty. - Zeitschrift fur Agyptische Sprache und Altertum vol.138, p169.

PART 2

THE 22nd, AND 23rd DYNASTIES

ABSTRACT

The 22nd and its 23rd Dynasty offshoot, will be argued, occupies the whole of the 3rd Intermediate Period, largely parallel with the 21st Priest King Dynasty.

The kings and their arrangement are here outlined, and argument will be made that these Dynasties embraced many parallel reigns.They cannot be explained by simple linear addition, and the claim will be made that these Dynasties began during the later declining years of Ramses II, the concept of a simple one pharaoh linear arrangement of the history of this period fails to explain the historical reality.

KEYWORDS.

Sheshonk, Orsorkon, Takelot, Harsiese, Pedubast, Pimay, Peftauawybast, Iuput, - names of kings of this period.

INTRODUCTION

Here we introduce the 22nd Dynasty, which it will be claimed and shown to have occupied the whole of the 'Third Intermediate Period', reigning alongside several other dynasties.

The 22nd Dynasty also gave rise to several subsidiary dynasties, the 23rd Dynasty and an alternate 23rd Dynasty, as well as kings of Herocleopolis Magna. Next, Manetho's 23rd Dynasty which followed the last kings of Dynasty 22, in Tanis as claimed, and mostly subsidiary to the 26th Dynasty.

Two important invasions occurred during the 22nd Dynasty:-

1) The attack by the Kushite king Piye (Piankhi), establishing the 25th Dynasty, and enabling us to set fixed points by the kings named. -This has already been dated to 711 BC approximately half way through the times of the 22nd Dynasty. This also will correspond with the beginning of the 24th Libyan Dynasty following the contemporary attack by Tefnakht 1.
2) The attack 47 years later by Assyrian Assurbanipal in 664 BC, also allowing us to identify certain kings.

The kings usually agreed upon conventionally during these two events are, for the most part, considered here to be largely incorrect and further identifications will be made during this presentation.

22ND DYNASTY

Seminal to understanding this period is this 22nd Dynasty, and this begins with "Sheshonk"- great chief of the Meshwesh, a term used for a major tribe of the Libyan people, just to the west of Egypt. (This group are almost certainly descendants of Lehabim, also called Lubim Gen. 10:13 and historically one of the known tribes was the Libu) One of the tribes descended from Mizraim father of the Egyptian people, but almost certainly migrating further west from Egypt.

We meet this person from the 'Sheshenk Stela' (Blackman,1941, p. 83-95), found at Abydos by Mariette.

He is universally believed to be Sheshonk I, founder of the 22nd Dynasty, which therefore is clearly of Libyan origin.

It is of interest that Orsorkon II, one of Sheshonk's descendants (Jacquet-Gordon, JEA, 1960, p.23), also acknowledged this origin.Stating he fears an adversary that he calls the 'pywd', (Biblical Phut)- the Berber speaking Libyans of classical history, a different group, and further west.

Returning to the Sheshonk Stela, we find a 'chief of the Meshwesh' (possibly the Maxyes of Herodotus -p.306) in control of an area around Heracleopolis (Ihnasya - Henen-nesut). Son of a certain Nimrat (Nemerat, Nimlot A), and clearly in favour with the reigning king, who is NOT identified, and ASSUMED by conventional chronology to be Psusennes II (Pesibhenno II) one of the last priest-kings of the 21st Dynasty. "Sheshonk' is clearly a powerful military leader, having an army under his control.

On the stela he is appealing to the king concerning a statue of his father, who also was apparently a military leader under the king.

Sheshonk, whose people appear to have been settled in Egypt for some time, most likely around the area of Heracleopolis, may well have received a posting in an official capacity to Bubastis or even Tanis, centres of much of his later dynasty.

However, by this revision, we will recognise the reigning king, not as Psusennes II, but Ramses II before his suggested incapacity, and the stela perhaps to be dated as early as 770 BC. David Rohl's findings -"A Test of Time"- of parallelism of the 21st and 22nd Dynasties, rule out the possibility of the king being Psusennes II.

Sheshonk I then came to power at a time of another King whom he acknowledged as overlord.

In Rohl's revision, he dates Ramses II earlier than is here being suggested, basing his dating on astronomical calculations. THAT means for dating is here rejected for any dates before 701 BC- the date that Hezekiah was given the 10 degree backward movement of the shadow on the Sundial of Ahaz (Isaiah 38:7-8), for such demands a small change of earth's axis and therefore would alter ALL astronomical calculations before 701 BC. As already mentioned, the dates here used for Ramses II are 792-727 BC.

Now we have historical synchronisms for the early 22nd Dynasty with the kings of Byblos, which Rohl has discussed:-

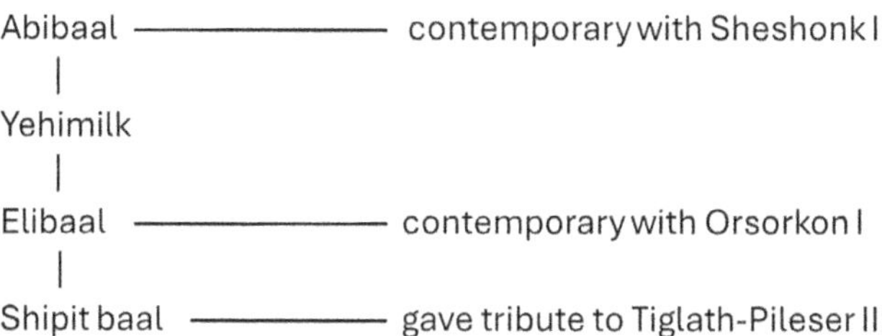

However, he admits the possibility that the order is :-(note 5-p. 419)

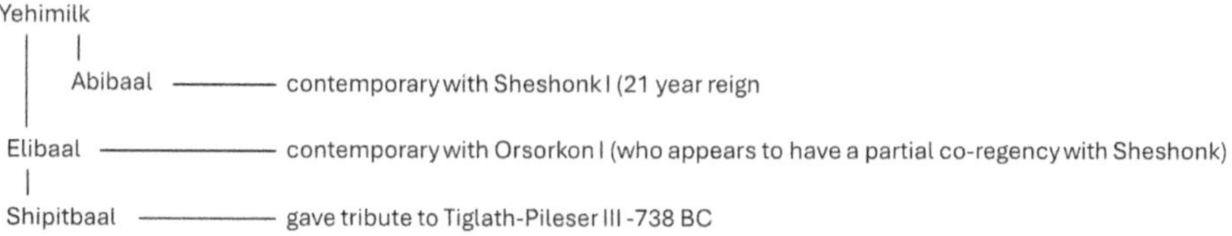

The most likely of the above genealogies, consistent with elapsed time, is the latter.

Added synchronism related to Ramses II:-

Further details emerge concerning this Dynasty of kings in Byblos, with the tomb of Ahiram.

The tomb contained a coffin made for his father Ahiram by Ethobaal (Pilsibaal) king of Byblos. The burial chamber also contained fragments of an alabaster jar, two fragments of which contained the cartouche of Ramses II (P. Montet, 1928, ch IV).

Now against the conventional chronology, the archaeologists have dated the tomb to the 13th century BC, but epigraphists insisted on a date much later and suggested that the inscription was close to those of Elibaal and Abibaal statues (see above). For which they suggest were somewhere between the Mesha Stele and Hezekiah's Siloam inscription.

Arguments have raged for several generations, with apparently the epigraphers recently prevailing.

Now on this revision we date Ramses II 792-727 BC, and an 8 year earlier co-regency (or more likely prince-regency) with Seti I.

The Mesha Stele close to 840 BC, probably written during the reign of Ahab's son Jehoram, (death of Ahab - 850 BC, 3 years after Qarqar - this is 3 years later than Thiele's claim). And the Hezekiah Siloam inscription 701 BC (but Hezekiah claimed the 17th year = 698 BC).

On this revision and consistent with archaeological details, we can place Abibaal and Elibaal inscriptions just around or before 750 BC, and the difference between these and the Ahiram inscription is small.

There is therefore good reason to list the Byblos 8th century dynasty as follows:-

?
Ahiram — Ethobaal — Yehimilk ├─ Abibaal
(Pilsibaal) └─ Elibaal

This would place Ahiram's tomb somewhere close to 800-780 BC and therefore would overlap the early days of Ramses II (whose cartouche was found there, and he would have been with his father Seti I in that area in early days). Giving reason to align the days of the beginning of the 22nd Dynasty during the time of Ramses II, and consistent with the dates given in this revision. The implication is profound- Sheshonk I is NOT Shishak of the Bible of the 10th century BC, regardless of the similarity of the names, nor can Ramses II be.

THE EARLY GENEALOGY OF SHESHONK -from the Pasenhor Stele

Buyuwawa "the Libyan"
|
Mawasun great chief
|
Nebneshi great chief
|
Paihut (Y) great chief
|
Sheshonk A=Mehtenweshet A
|
Nimot A=Tentsepeh A
|
SHESHONK I   Great chief of the Ma
Hedjkheperre setepenre Sheshonk – throne name
(Sheshonk B) Shesheneq mery Amun – birth name.
Horus – Ka nakht mery Re sekhaef em nesu er sema tawy
Strong bull beloved of Ra, who the latter has caused to unit the 2 lands.
Nebty – Ka em sekhemty mi Hor sa Aset sehetep netjeru em maat.
Who has appeared in the double crown like Horus the son of Isis and pacified the gods with maat.

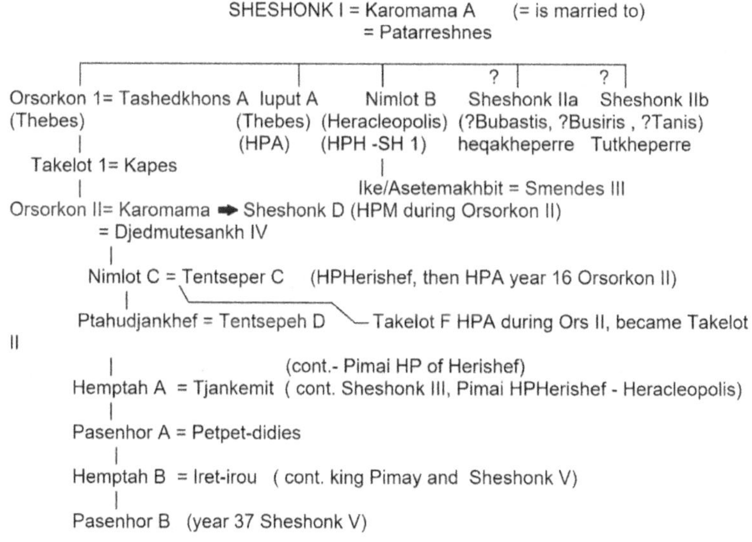

The present author rejects the claim that this genealogy cannot be taken in the linear fashion as presented.As the discussion proceeds, it will become evident that the linear arrangement does in fact fit the spread of the 22nd Dynasty.

THE KINGS OF THE 22nd DYNASTY

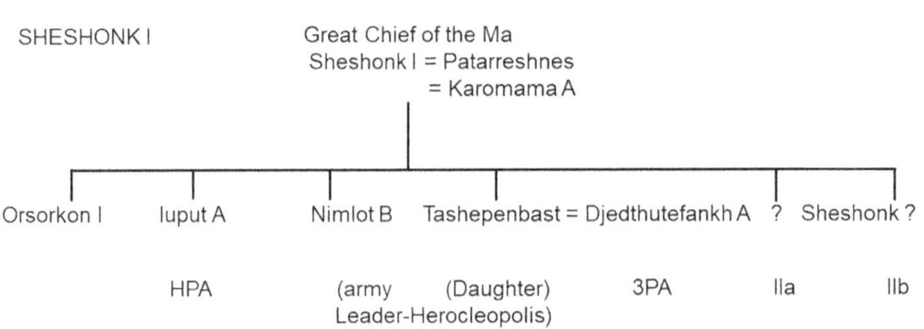

Sheshonk's reign of 21 years almost certainly involved co-regencies with his sons. He himself married off his daughter Tashepenbast to a Djedthutefankh A, a third prophet of Amun at Thebes, and called King's son of Ramses.

SHESHONK'S SONS:-

1) Iuput A who was high priest of Amun in Thebes during his reign.

   Iuput would marry off his daughter Neskhonspakhered to son of a Theban priestly family - Djedkhonsefankh A, fourth prophet of Amun, indicating a closeness in time of Sheshonk I and family to the priestly hierarchy in Thebes. These relationships were very important in subsequent events.
2) Nimlot B "Leader of the Army", Priest of Herishef, in Heracleopolis appealed to Sheshonk I about sacrifices to the local god.

Apparently, he had a daughter Ike/Asetemakhbit who became consort to nephew Smendes III HPA, and possibly a son Orsorkon (Perez Die 2007- Orsorkon 5 of excavation)

3) Orsorkon I, by the conventional accepted chronology, was married to a Maatkare, as a result of the genealogy found by a 'Sheshonk HPA' on the nile-god statue BM 8, but this has come under serious question and may not in fact refer to Orsorkon I, and therefore Orsorkon I may not have had a son Sheshonk, nor in fact married Maatkare.

However, it is clear that Orsorkon I was a king of some significance, controlling the areas around Heracleopolis. He worked on Sheshonk I's temple at El-Hibeh (Kitchen 263) and built a fortress north of Heracleopolis called Pi-Sekhemkheperre. Thus while the other brothers were co-ruling contemporary with Sheshonk I, it is inconceivable that Orsorkon I was not so. It may well be that the 15 years attributed by Manetho simply is the sole reign after Sheshonk's death, although we have no certainty of this.

Orsorkon I's highest year date known was thought to be 36 years (Petrie, p. 241), but Jacquet Gordon has shown this to be a misreading (JEA 53 p63-1967). At present 33 is believed to be the highest date (on linen on body of a priest in the Ramessaeum, associated with braces having a *menat*-tab of Orsorkon I - Quibell The Ramessaeum 1898 10-11). This has been questioned, but considering the details of the reign of Orsorkon I, he appears to have been a significant king, and significant builder.

Some have suggested that the 15 years was a mistake for 35 years by Manetho, but considering a very likely significant co-regency, Manetho's figure should be taken seriously.

The co-regency is strongly suggested by a cartouche containing both the names of Sheshonk I and Orsorkon I (Petrie Vol III, p.243)

Sheshonk I appears to have been of mature age when he began his tenure and dying at around 70 years of age is not unlikely. Having children born slightly before he was 20 years also is not unlikely, so that his children also would have significant maturity when he came to the throne (this is suggested by the burial of Sheshonk

IIa, who appears to be his son, dying early in Sheshonk I's reign but reaching into his 50's - by forensic examination).

The political circumstances alluded to earlier (Part 1), lent themselves to Sheshonk placing family members in as many places as possible, and both he and his son Iuput married daughters into the Theban priestly hierarchy. Overall giving Sheshonk's line a powerful voice in the Theban aristocracy.

However, Manetho alludes to three other kings in line, listed after Orsorkon I and before Takelot (Takelot I or II is not certain), and three names have come to attention - Sheshonk IIa (Sh IIa), (*heqakheperre setepenre*), who in fact appears most likely a son of Sheshonk I (buried as a secondary burial in the tomb of Psusennes I), forensic examination suggests that he died in his fifties, reigning briefly ? 2 years. Then another whose name has been found on Bubastis temple *Tutkheperre* Sheshonk IIb (Sh IIb), and also on ostracon E. 1886 found at Abydos, (again I suggest another son of Sheshonk I), and on a block found at Bubastis, who also appears to have reigned briefly ? 2-3 years.These two at Bubastis, Busiris or Tanis, perhaps at the same time as Orsorkon I's early years in Thebes, his burial suggests a closenes to the time of Harsiese A, and I suggest he and Sheshonk IIa may well have been followed by Orsorkon's son Takelot I (9 or 14 years), on their deaths. A third labelled Sheshonk IIc - *Maakheperre* is also known and on Cairo Stela CG42192 is said to be son of Psusennes (so he would be much later - but very likely the person mentioned by Aidan Dodson JEA 79 1993, p. 267-268, Theban tomb 18). These 3 Sheshonks are little understood, some believing that they are titles for the same Pharaoh, but most believe them to be separate individuals. This latter is accepted here until otherwise indicated, and it is suggested that Sheshonk IIa and b are likely early sons of Sheshonk I, perhaps given regional responsibilities co-regentally (with the exclusion of Sheshonk IIc who will be dealt with later).

AREA of RULE

While the 22nd Dynasty is said by Manetho to consist of 9 kings of Bubastis, the evidence would more likely place their ORIGIN at Heracleopolis magna, and LATER controlling Bubastis, then other cities especially Tanis. Troy L.Sagrillo (2009) has argued for Sheshonk I mainly from Heracleopolis and a fortress close to Mit Rahina near Memphis and possibly buried there. He also built a temple at El-Hibeh. Bubastis then seems to have become important under Orsorkon I and II soon after, but also perhaps occupied by Sheshonk IIb. Then came Tanis especially with Sheshonk III.

TAKELOT I
Throne name - Hedjkheperre setepenre
radiant one of the manifestations of Ra, chosen by Ra
Birth name - Takelot mery Amun

The evidence seems strong that Takelot I was in fact the son of Orsorkon I, by wife Tashedkhonsu (Pasenhor Stela), but would have been born very early to Orsorkon I, in order for his son Orsorkon II to begin his early reign in Tanis / Bubastis, contemporary with Orsorkon I in Pi-sekhemkheperre and influential in Thebes. (This is indicated by the fact that the inner hall of the temple of Bubastis was built by Orsorkon II (son of Tak.I), and the outer court was constructed by Orsorkon I (Rohl, 1995, p.377))

Takelot I was the father of Orsorkon II and the latter would have then reigned, following, in either Bubastis and Tanis (and Busiris), again slightly overlapping the reign of Orsorkon I, (it is my conviction that Orsorkon II is the Orsorkon in Bubastis during the invasion of Piye, but a very aged king at that time).

Takelot I's highest year date was year 14, but he appears to only have reigned in Tanis, but his tenure was overshadowed by his father Orsorkon I, with whom he appears to have reigned parallel, apparently dying before the latter. Then succeeded by son Orsorkon II, who then appears to have been in his early years parallel with Orsorkon I.

REIGN CORRELATION -overlap Sheshonk 1, Orsorkon 1, Takelot 1, early Orsorkon II

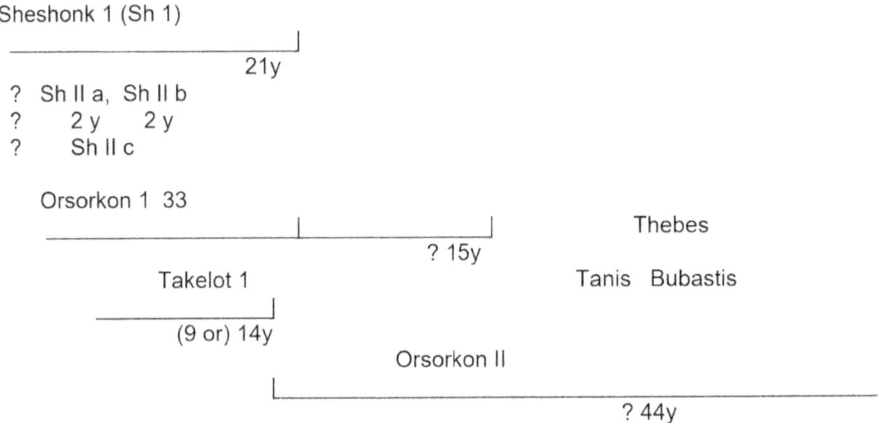

This overlap suggests that the linear passage of time between the start of reign of Sheshonk I and end of the total reigns of Orsorkon I and Takelot I, could not have been more than 35-40 years, depending on the time of co-regency between Sheshonk I and Orsorkon I.

Such a scenario is eminently possible if Sheshonk I already had several of his children well before he came to power. And each of the children before Takelot I having adult status. Takelot I himself also born to Orsorkon I just before Sheshonk began his rule. We now know that Orsorkon II reigned possibly up to 44-45 years (Aston) and therefore was quite young on coming to the throne.

ORSORKON I (Sekhem kheperre Orsorkon meryamun)
Horus name – Ka nakht meryre redjen sa itenu her nesetef er ergereg tawy
(The strong bull beloved of Ra, whom Atum put on the throne to establish the 2 lands)
Birth name — Orsorkon meryamun Orsorkon beloved of Amun.

This king was likely first at Heracleopolis, but clearly began association with Bubastis as was his grandson Orsorkon II. He built the fortress Pi-Sekhemkheperre north of Heracleopolis, which may have served as his main residence, but clearly able to place his sons Iuwelot then Smendes III as High Priests (HPA) at Thebes (Karnak) while he was alive.. Therefore he had some control of that city, following his father's earlier appointment of Iuput as HPA there. The father and son thus had secured a stronghold on that city then, controlling the High Priesthood and filial relations with both 3rd and 4th prophet families of that city (at Karnak).

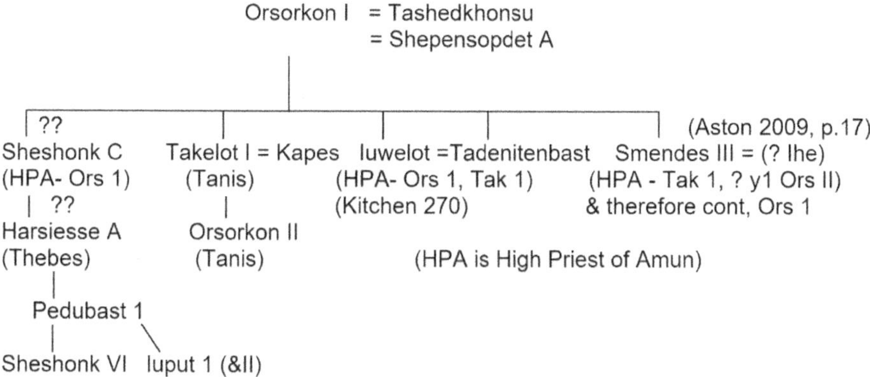

Smendes III HPA = Ihe/Asetemakhbit apparently daughter of Nimlot B (son of Sheshonk I) (Carmen Perez Die 2007 p.307 n. 21), or less likely daughter of Sheshonk I

SHESHONK C - ?

This genealogy is the conventional, and includes Sheshonk C who is claimed to be the son of Maatkare B daughter of Psusennes II, and is dependant on the claims made concerning the inscription of the statue of the Nile-god BM 8 (British Museum), and as Kitchen claimed (p. 60) "At one stroke, this provides a vital link between the 21st and 22nd Dynasties, long famed: the daughter of Psusennes II was married-off to Orsorkon (I), son of Sheshonq I who succeeded Psusennes II."

However, serious difficulties attend this claim, not least the Tanis burials which give reason to believe that the 21st and 22nd Dynasties were in fact contemporary (Rohl). Also by the fact that BM 8 does not identify the Orsorkon involved, nor demand that the Sheshonq (HPA here),who is the main subject of the statue, is in fact this Sheshonk conventionally labelled Sheshonq C, nor is there any other definitive evidence that Orsorkon I married a Maatkare.

Earlier Sheshonk here was believed to be the HPA who then became Sheshonk II. This idea lost favour, but has recently been revived by Rohl, with the difference that he appears to see this Sheshonk as a son of Orsorkon II, and then the following HPA's to Takelot F (Takelot II) being descendants.

This presents other problems, because during Talelot II's reign a conflict developed with the original family, after Harsiese A, when Orsorkon II placed his son Nimlot C as HPA at Thebes, and his grandson Takelot F HPA on the Theban throne as Takelot II, laying the foundation for conflict between two families, and Rohl's suggestion gives no logic to a interfamily conflict.

BM 8 would fit better with Sheshonk HPA (alias Sheshonk C) being a son of a later Orsorkon with possible consort Maatkara B (Porter -private communication favours Orsorkon III, but a different individual will be put forward here later). There is in fact no certain evidence that Orsorkon I ever had a wife called Maatkare, nor that there was a Sheshonk C HPA at Thebes at the claimed time, this is a result of a faulty conventional chronology.

Orsorkon II, initially contemporary with Harsiese A, placed son Nimlot C as HPA at Thebes (no doubt after Smendes III), followed soon by grandson Takelot F.On the death of Harsiese A elevating grandson Takelot F to the status of king at Thebes -Takelot II, and usurping the throne from a young Pedubast, with soon resultant conflict.

Pedubast (I) regained the throne, then his son Iuput I (and II see later) reigned, followed by brother Sheshonk VI, then Iny, while Iuput moved to Leontopolis.

Orsorkon B (son of Takelot II then soon called Orsorkon III) regained the throne in the 39th year of Sheshonk III, reigning for 28 years.

The conclusion then is that the family leading to Harsiese A (king) could be direct descendants of Orsorkon I through son Smendes III, then conflicting with the other branch of the family via Sheshonk I's great grandson Orsorkon II - as follows:-

In 2009, p 17 (from 2007), Aston added information that may solve this problem.

In a royal necropolis at Heracleopolis (likely origin of the Bubastite Dynasty - Sagrillo, 2007), Aston mentions the finding of a 'Tenetamun' 'chief of the Harim of Concubines of Herishef', daughter of a HPA Smendes (almost certainly III), and sister of a king which is, considering time and place, likely Harsiese A. That would give the following:-

__Iuput I

Iuput I
HPA's
Iuput A HPA(son of Sheshonk I)
(Pedubast) — Sheshonk VI
(Orsorkon I) → Iuwelot HPA, & Smendes III HPA
(–du)
Iny
HPA
Harsiese B
(Harsiese A) = ? Shebensopdet
HPA
Tenetamun
Takelot I
Istweret = Harsiese C
Takelot II, usurpation
Orsorkon II
(2 then 4PA)
Nimlot C HPA → Takelot F HPA

This solution then posits that the 2 lines known to us as the 23rd Dynasty were opposing lines who conflicted, such created by separate aspirations of two cousins, namely Orsorkon II and Harsiese A, both grandsons of Orsorkon I. Each line representing a break-off line from the 22nd Dynasty.

Unlike Aston, however, I would see Pedubast 'Si-ese, and Si-bast' as the same, bearing in mind ancestry of Orsorkon I with Bubastis, and Pedubast's rule at Thebes, I simply don't see any conflict with these two epithets.

An addition would see the assumption (very briefly) of Pedubast as HPA (—du/'awti) just before the usurpation of the Theban throne by Takelot II

IUWELOT HPA

This son of Orsorkon I was made HPA, most likely following Iuput A (son of Sheshonk I), and was married to sister Tadenitenbast, his daughter Djedeseesankh married 3PA Padimut ii (Patjenfy), begetting a Djedkhonsefankh.

SMENDES III HPA

Became HPA after brother Iuwelot, and apparently married Ihe/Asetemakhbit (Divine mother, = mother of the king) a daughter of Nimlot B (son of Sheshonk I), became father of Harsiese A (the latter ? married to a Shepensopdet). Daughter of Smendes and sister of Harsiese A was Tanetamun (chief of the harim -ladies of Herishef at Heracleopolis)-her daughter Tanetsheritieniah (Imyt bah priest of Herishef - celibate).

Aston 2014 also suggests a wife Istemkheb.

Smendes may also have had a wife Tchysetch by whom he had a son Orsorkon. This latter son known by the excavators at Heracleopolis Magna (3rd Intermediate period) as Orsorkon 3 (and possibly 4 and 2), called "king's son of Ramses", "great chief of Pi-sekhemkheperre", "prophet of Herishef", "general and commander of troops".

The title "King's son of Rameses" meaning is not agreed upon, but one idea is that it represents direct descendants of the Ramesides through the female line. In that it is worth appreciating that this title has been applied to 3 Orsorkons found at the Heracleopolis Magna necropolis. This may represent only two separate Orsorkons, likely sons of Smendes III HPA, and Nimlot C HPH and HPA. but the title also was associated with Psusennes I and son - i.e. Ramesses -Psusennes and son Ramesses- Ankhefenmut (and here we know of the D.H.Henttawy A, mother of Psusennes I and daughter of Ramesses XI and wife of Khakheperre Pinudjem I). These later would be close contemporaries of the subjects of the above mentioned necropolis.

If such could be shown to be the case, it would undoubtedly increase the here presented revision where the early 21st and early 22nd Dynasties are contemporary with the 20th Dynasty, and the Ramesides most likely of the 20th Dynasty.

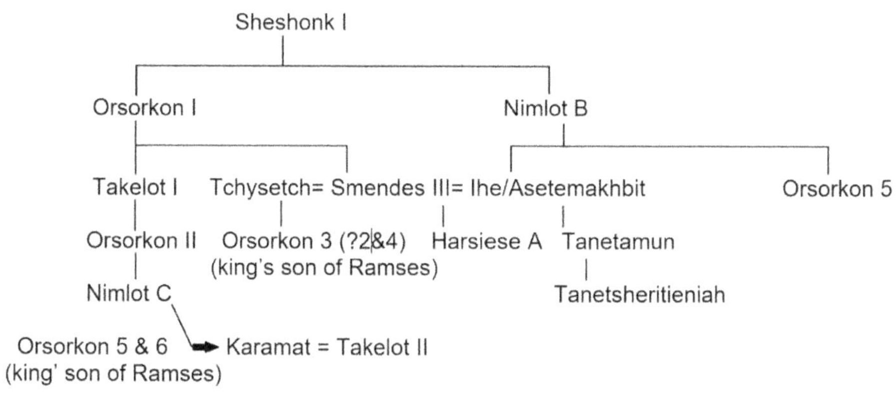

TAKELOT I (see above)

ORSORKON II son of Takelot I

HORUS - *Ka nakht mery maat* - strong bull beloved of maat

ka nakht mery maat,sekha su ra er nesu - strong bull beloved of maat, whom Ra caused to be king of the two lands.

ka nakht kha em Waset - strong bull who has appeared in Thebes.

NEBTY - *Sema peseshty mi sa Aset, demedjef sekhemty em hetep* - The one who has united the two lands like the son of Isis he has assembled.

Sema peseshty mi sa Aset, sehet netjeru em iret maat - The one who has united the two lands like the son of Isis, who has satisfied the gods by performing Maat.

Sema peseshty mi sa Aset, demedj.en.ef sekhemty em hetep - The one who has united the two lands like the son of Isis has assembled the two crowns in peace.

GOLDEN HORUS - *Wer pehty, hui mentjyu, user*—The mighty one who has struck down the bedouin, rich—

Wer pehty, der setjtui, user fau em tau nebu. - The great of strength one who has repelled the Setjetui-Asiatics is rich in splendour in all lands.

Sekhem pehty, huikheftyuef, user fau - The mighty powerful one who has struck down his enemies in rich splendour.

—der pedjet, ity, sekhem em tau nebu - who has repelled the (foreign) bowmen, the mighty sovereign in all lands.

THRONE - *Usermaatre setepenamun* - strong one belonging to the Maat of Ra.

Alternate *(Usermaatre setepenre)*

BIRTH - *Userken sa Bastet meryamun (Meryre)* - Osorkon son of Bastet, beloved of Amun (beloved of Ra)

(—sa Bastet connects him to Bubastis, kha em Waset connects him to Thebes).

It is my conviction that this kings reign has been severely underestimated, but in recent years the tenure of his reign has been verified (particularly Aston 1989). Orsorkon can now be seen as the most powerful Pharaoh of the 22nd Dynasty, possibly reigning up to 44-45 years, his early years overlapping those of Orsorkon I - his grandfather and then overlapping the early reigns of several of his sons. Then securing both Upper and lower Egypt for his descendants, and hence the progenitor of both the Theban 23rd Dynasty and the balance of the 22nd Dynasty at Tanis. This seems to be reflected in one of his Nebty name variants:-

Sema peseshty mi sa Aset demedy, en. ef sekhemty em hetep dehen...

(The one who has united the two lands, like the son of Isis has assembled the two crowns in peace whom god [x] appointed ...)

Aston has shown that this king overlapped several generations of his contemporaries and was ancestor to the residual 22nd Dynasty Tanite Throne and the 23rd Theban throne. Placing his grandson Takelot II on the Theban throne (previously Takelot F HPA), temporarily displacing the line of his cousin Harsiese A (and son Pedubast HPA .du/'awti -Legrain 1905, Jacquet - Gordon 1967), which then reasserted, and provoking a civil war in the family.

Placing likely son Sheshonk III on the Tanite throne, and likely son Rudamun in Heracleopolis. Son Nimlot C would be High Priest of Herishef in Heracleopolis until Orsorkon's year 16 when he would be made High Priest of Amun at Thebes. But the line continuing with rulers of Heracleopolis down to Pasenhor B.

Orsorkon would also place son and crown Prince Sheshonk D as High Priest of Ptah at Memphis, controlling that line for several generations.

Aston has argued that Orsorkon II may have lived over 40 years of reign contemporary with 4 generations of officials including 4th Prophet of Amun (4PA) Nakhtefmut A who also officiated under Orsorkon III (previously Orsorkon B HPA - his great grandson), but probably Orsorkon II died before Orsorkon III assumed the throne.

If Aston's estimation of Orsorkon II's age is close to correct and the Orsorkon at Bubastis on the Piankhi Stela is correct, then Orsorkon would have come to the throne perhaps around 43 years before Piankhi (711 BC- 30th year of Sheshonk III), then his year of accession would be circa. 754 BC., i.e. 9 years before the accession of Tiglath-Pileser III in Assyria, just before the 38 / 39th year of Uzziah of Judah, and the year that Zechariah son of Jeroboam II of Israel came to the throne.

This date of Orsorkon II give credence to Courville's claim that Sheshonk I, Orsorkon I and Orsorkon II, overlapped sufficiently for participation in the same wars (P. 323). Namely Sheshonk I's attack into Palestine, which I later suggest would be 750 BC, during the early reign of Menahem.

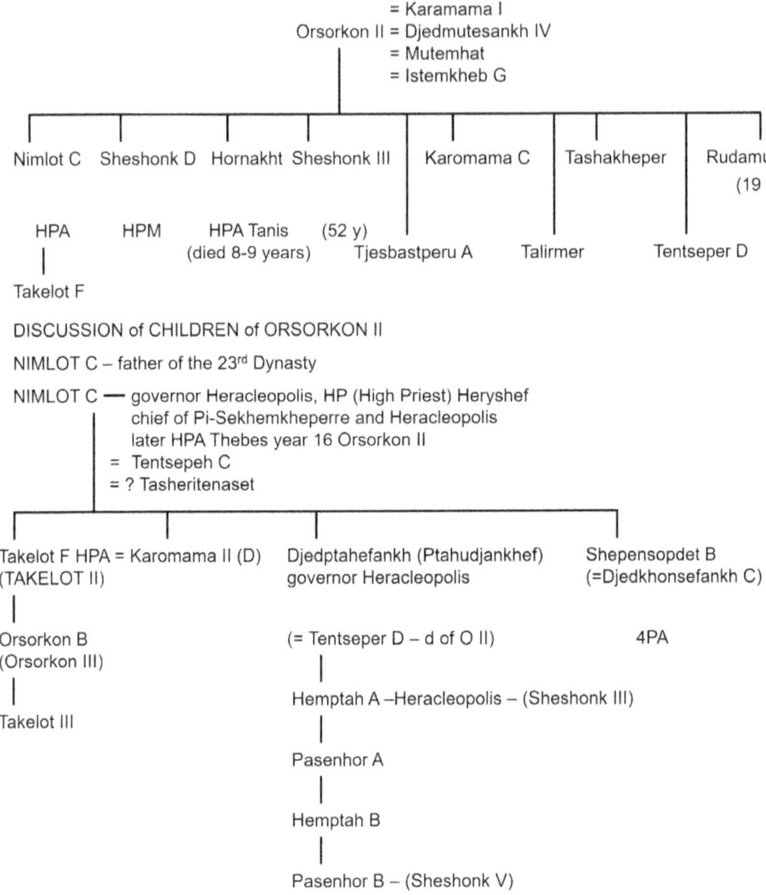

Also, son Orsorkon -priest of Herishef, chief of army, son of King's son of 'lord of the 2 lands, Cairo (JE94736), and tomb 1 royal necropolis Heracleopolis Magna, (perhaps the same as the Orsorkon 5 & 6 mentioned by Perez Die 2007).

As well as Tcheretch by Tasheritenaset

SHESHONK D

Placed as HP of Ptah Memphis (HPM) but predeceasing his father.

I believe this person has been confused with his brother Sheshonk III in terms of his genealogy. In Memorial stone - year 28 of Sheshonk III- of Ped-ise and sons

Peftjauawybast and Takelot (D),- the father of Takelot B father of Ped-ise is said to be Sheshonk entitled "his majesty", who can only be Sheshonk III at that moment and is called a son of Orsorkon II, and brother therefore of Sheshonk D HPM. We therefore have no certain descendant genealogy of Sheshonk D.

HORNAKHT

Orsorkon placed this son as HPA at Tanis, however he died young -about 8-9 years old.

SHESHONK III - we will deal later with this significant king, but he logically almost certainly should be accepted as a son of Orsorkon II (Memorial Stone of the satrap Pediese and his sons Peftatbast and Takelot) and placed in Tanis 3 years after the accession of Takelot II in Thebes.

RUDAMUN

This king has been attributed as a son of Orsorkon III, by speculation, against the conventional chronology which assumes Piye's invasion during the sole reign of Sheshonk V. However soon discussion will associate him earlier and therefore almost certainly a younger son of Orsorkon II, and younger brother of Sheshonk III, placed in Heracleopolis.

SOME SUGGESTED CONCLUSIONS

The evidence would suggest that Takelot I was Orsorkon I's son born to Tashedkhonsu.

Takelot I would be followed by his young son Orsorkon II almost certainly before the death of Takelot's father Orsorkon I and have a long and powerful reign that would change the power balance for his descendants.

Following Orsorkon I Harsiese A (*Hedjkheperre setepenamun*) would take the throne in Thebes, however Orsorkon placed Iuwelot HPA, then Smendes III as

HPA (father of Harsiese A) in Thebes. During Harsiese reign his son ...du/'awti would also briefly be HPA, followed by Orsorkon II's son Nimlot C as HPA year 16 of Orsorkon II, and by Takelot F - HPA (later Takelot II), son of Nimlot C at Thebes, whether this was by consent or coercion is not certain but may have been the second.

The evidence would then allow that on the death of Harsiese A, Orsorkon II would appoint his grandson Takelot II at Thebes (Aston 1989), (the latter having already served as HPA Takelot F), and before him son Nimlot C at Heracleopolis then Thebes, indicating essentially a takeover in Upper Egypt by that branch of the family, while Orsorkon II himself continued to rule at Tanis / Bubastis / Busiris.

A SYNCHRONISM

Orsorkon II's rule (which was a long one) finds a close synchronism with the later years of Northern Israel, as a vase bearing his cartouche was found in the palace in Samaria. The find has provoked debate, but this is clearly associated with one of the kings FOLLOWING Jeroboam II of Northern Israel, as suggested by unstated author at www.vararchive.org:

> *"The conclusion has now for some time been generally accepted that the Samaritan ostraca were written not in Ahab's time but in the time of the last kings of Samaria. Of the kings of Israel after Ahab, only Jeroboam II and Pekah reigned more than seventeen years—the ostraca were written in the days of Jeroboam II,—This conclusion appears to be correct.*

And:

> *"The house that sheltered the jar of Orsorkon II in Samaria was built on the ruins of the house that sheltered the inscribe potsherds—. Judged by the findings, Orsorkon II was not only later than Ahab, but also later than Jeroboam II."*

Although this author is not correct in ascribing more than 17 years only to Jeroboam and Pekah, the point made is that the ostraca belong to the end period of Northern Israel.

The ostraca have been said to be close to the Siloam Inscription, and that is dated to Hezekiah, in his 17th year 698 BC.

Moreover Matthew J. Suriano - "Biblical Odyssey" has claimed they belong to the end period of Jehu's Dynasty.

The likely Israelite king here would be the Anti-Assyrian Pekah (the previous king Menahem being an acknowledged Assyrian vassal under Tiglath-Pileser III, - ARAB 1-772), for Orsorkon II well knew that the Assyrian war-machine was on the march.

Later we will associate Sheshonk III, son of Orsorkon II with the next ruler, Hoshea king of Israel, the "king So" of Tanis to whom Hoshea appealed (2 Kings 17:4), in the days of Shalmaneser V of Assyria (most likely 725 or 726 BC, v. 5).

A second reason for placing Orsorkon II with the later years of Northern Israel's kings is consequent upon the details arrived earlier regarding the Byblos kings, the synchronisms arrived at there demand Orsorkon II in close relation in time to the reign of Tiglath Pileser III of Assyria (745 - 727 BC).

RUDAMUN

Usermaatre setepenamun Rudamun meryamun

Little is known of this pharaoh who has been associated with Heracleopolis (Aston).

He is believed, by the conventional chronology, to be a son of Orsorkopn III and younger brother of Takelot III.

Such a conclusion, however, distorts the time -line, for Rudamun was one generation before Peftjauawybast who was an HPM and later King in Heracleopolis, parallel with Sheshonk III (Sh III), who himself is parallel with Takelot II during his (Sh III) early years.

Apis Stela identifies Peftjauawybast as HPM during the 28th year of Sheshonk III, i.e. 6 years after the death of Takelot II, father of Orsorkon III, the latter coming to the throne 11 years later (39th year of Sheshonk III) and reigning for 28 years. And although such a time-line could be argued, the ages involved sit uncomfortably with the facts.

Rudamun then sits parallel during the reign of Sheshonk III and therefore can reasonably be understood as a younger son of Orsorkon II, placed on the Heracleopolitan throne by Orsorkon II several years after Sheshonk III was enthroned in Tanis. And Sheshonk III was enthroned 3 years after his nephew Takelot II (formerly HPA Takelot F in Thebes, and son of Orsorkon's older son Nimlot C) was placed on the theban throne by Orsorkon II.

I therefore place Rudamun as a younger son of Orsorkon II and brother of Sheshonk III and Nimlot C, and as Aston has made a strong case for a long life for Orsorkon II, Rudamun could well have been born a number of years after Nimlot C and Sheshonk III.

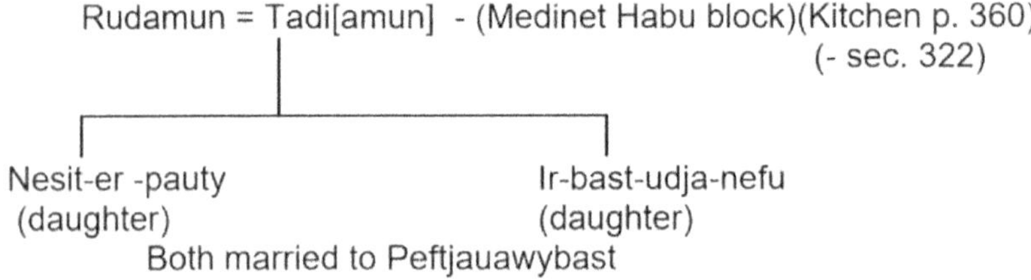

PEFTJAUAWYBAST HPM then KING

Neferkare

Present during attack by Piye, and there called 'king' of Heracleopolis, this event is dated here to 711 BC, circa. year 30 of Sheshonk III.

Direct descendant of Orsorkon II

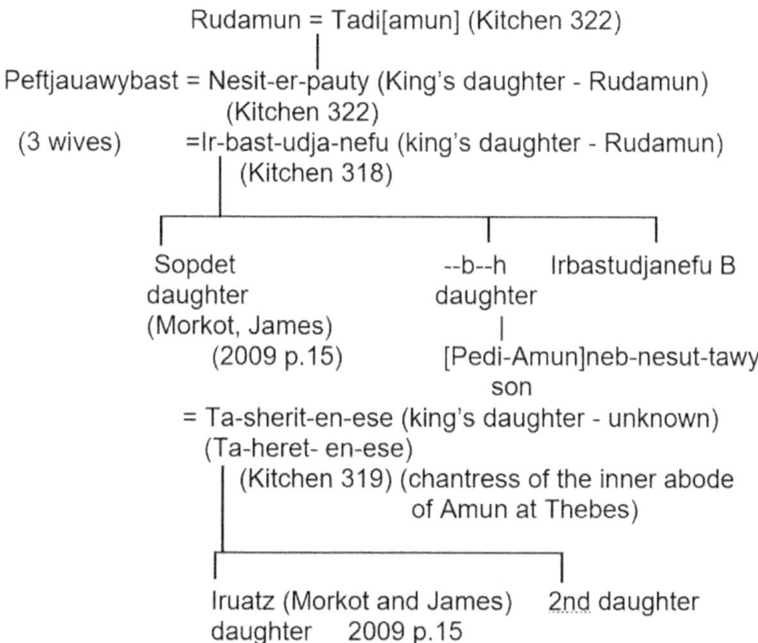

PEFTAUAWYBAST
Rey de nen-nesut King of Heracleopolis
Peftjauawybast wi Bast In the hands of Bastet
Peftjauawybast Neferkare sa Re son of Ra.

Let us follow the line to Peftauawybast, son-in-law to Rudamun, during whose reign (a possible at least 10 + years) Plye invaded. This man was well connected to the royal line, marrying 3 'king's daughters'.

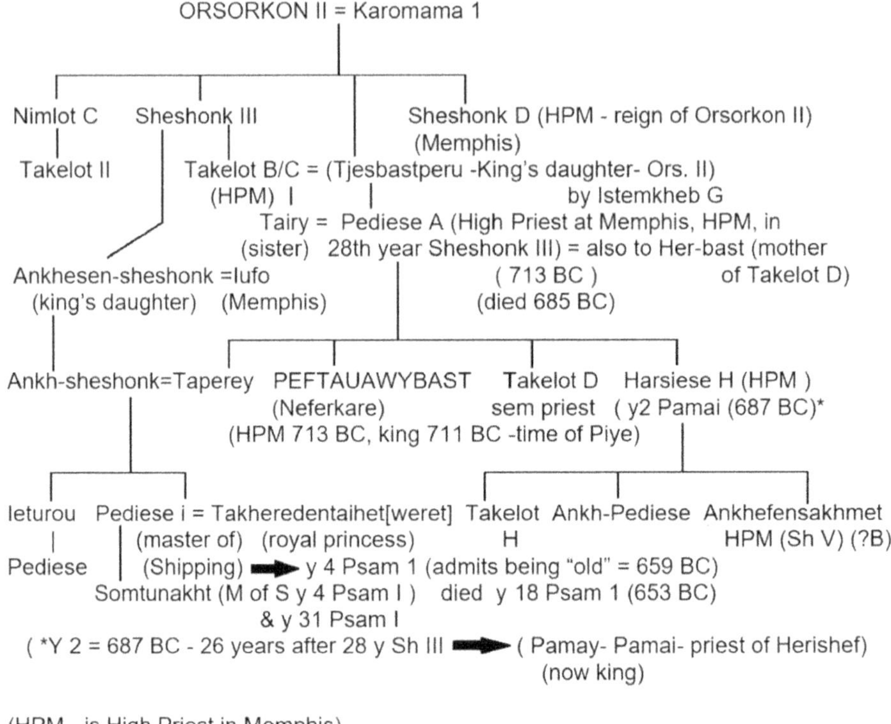

(HPM - is High Priest in Memphis)

It should be noted, by the records at the Serapaeum, that Peftauawybast was contemporary with Sheshonk III's later years, but Harsiese H (brother) appears to have been HPM after Peftauawybast, ? after the latter started rule at Heracleopolis.

RELEVANT APIS STELAE

Three Apis Stelae clarify the situation

1) Stela set up in year 2 of King Pamai in memory of HPM Pediese, tells us that at that moment Sheshonk III was dead, and Pediese had been involved in year 28 of Sheshonk III with the instillation of the Apis bull, in associa-

tion with Peftauawybast HPM, and Takelot D, priest of Ptah and brother of the latter.

2) Apis stela set up by Harsiese HPM (brother) year 2 Pamai, stating burial of the Apis bull, having had 26 years lifetime, installed 28th year of Sheshonk by Pediese.

3) Apis stela set up by Harsiese H in year 2 Pamai in memory of his father Pediese HPM, who at the time of Sheshonk III, installed Apis in 28th year of Sheshonk III.

These stela tell us that Sheshonk's 28th year was a time when Pediese was HPM and Peftauawybast was HPM, not yet king, although the third of these calls Pediese 'general' and Peftauawybast HPM. Kitchen (p.193-4) says;- "This conjunction suggests that Pediese—had installed his son in office with himself, perhaps to relieve him of priestly duties and to secure the family claims to the office."

The stelae also confirm that Sheshonk III was son of Orsorkon II must have indeed reigned for 52 years, (unless solid evidence to the contrary exists).

4) Stela from from Satrap Pediese and sons Peftjauwybasy and Takelot - in 28th year of Sheshonk III, son of Takelot and Tjestashperu, son of MAJESTY Sheshonk son of Orsorkon II. This stelae is pivotal, for not only does it mention Takelot B (and almost certainly the same as C), as the son of Majesty Sheshonk (in 28th year of Sheshonk III), but claims Sheshonk as son of Orsorkon (II), thus not referring to Sheshonk D. In the same stela Peftjauwybast and brother Takelot D are mentioned, clearly placing Peftjauwybast, Takelot D contemporary with Sheshonk III' 28th year, and allowing the possibility that Orsorkon II could also still be alive, as I have inferred in re-interpretation of the Piankhi Stela.

As Pedubast I's last year Y 23 corresponds to year 30 of Sheshonk III, and Pedubast 1 finds no mention on the Piye Stele, but Iuput does (stationed at Leontoplois, his brother Sheshonk VI clearly ready to take charge at Thebes, but not mentioned by Piye), at which stage also Peftauawybast is 'king' (at Heracleopolis), we would have to place Piye' s invasion (year 711BC) after or at the end of Sheshonk's 30th year, but almost certainly not long after this.

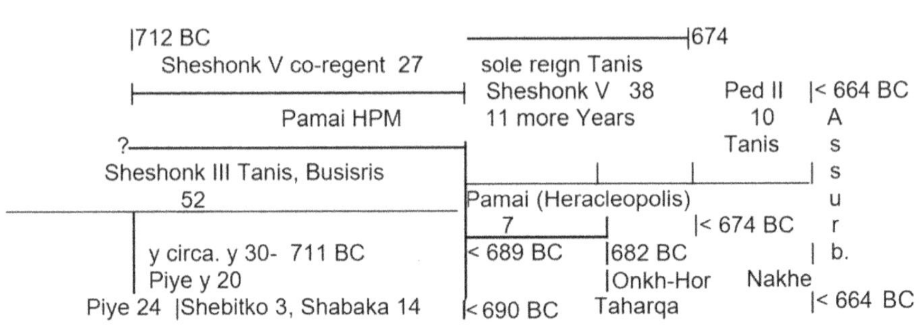

Returning to Orsorkon II, he is seen on reliefs at Temple J at Karnak "as a celebrant, whilst on the facade, his grandson, Takelot F is shown as High Priest of Amun—" (Aston p.147) Takelot F was High Priest earlier during reign of Orsorkon II and went on to become Takelot II ruling at Thebes, contemporary with Orsorkon II. Three years after Takelot II's accession Orsorkon II elevated his son Sheshonk III to throne at Tanis / Bubastis / Busiris, and very likely Rudamun to ruler of Heracleopolis a few years later.

If we are to use Aston's suggestions of Rudamun's place in relation to Pedftauawybast, (1989 p.153) we need to remove 5 years for Iny who in fact reigned at Thebes (not Heracleopolis), then Rudamun came to the throne 19 + years before 711 BC (Piye's invasion), so circ. 730 - 732 BC, and so after Sheshonk III's accession circa. 741 BC (provisional), placing Takelot II's accession at circa. 744 BC (provisional) - perhaps a couple of years later may be possible. Overall, it appears that Piye attacked around Sheshonk III's 30th year

It is very likely that the Orsorkon of Bubastis on the Piye stela is an aged Orsorkon II in Bubastis, Sheshonk is almost certainly Sheshonk III, although it is possible that Sheshonk V may have just become co-regent at that moment, or straight after Piye's attack.

It is of interest that M.L. Bierbrier (The Late New Kingdom in Egypt- ch 4) associates Peftauawybast not with Sheshonk V as many others, but with Sheshonk

III, certainly while he was HPM, and close to the time of HPA Orsorkon B, and therefore also Sheshonk III.

As Peftauawybast - Neferkare, has been recognised as a king but earlier as HPM, a likely order of his reign would be just after Sheshonk IV (Haq An - ruler of Heliopolis), which would allow the possibility that Rudamun ruled parallel with Sheshonk IV, but in Heracleopolis.

Such would give a rule of Kings co-regent with Sheshonk III, in HERACLEOPOLIS - Rudamun -19y, Peftauawybast -10y- between 730 and 701 BC, and in HELIOPOLIS - Sheshonk IV - 'Haq An' (6 or 10 y) (?at or before 719-713 BC), Sheshonk V- 'Haq An', at the early part his reign (712-674 BC see later during discussion of 24th Dynasty).

PHARAOH INY -*Si-ese meryamun*

However, this king whom some scholars place in Heracleopolis between Rudamun and Peftauawybast, is known as "Iny Si-ese Meryamun".Such suggests that he in fact reigned in Thebes, not Heracleopolis, his highest year is 5, while the other king after Pedubast at that period is Sheshonk VI highest year date 6 year, but both being found mentioned at Karnak by father and son dignitaries.

If the 6th year of Sheshonk VI is only a fraction of a year, it would explain the period of 10 years missing by Orsorkon B before he regained Thebes:- i.e. Sheshonk VI - 5 and a fraction of the 6th year, plus Iny to a 5th year but not complete = 10 years.

So Pedubast 23 years followed by Sheshonk VI (son) then Iny (? brother)- the last two =10 years. Iuput 1 (the other likely brother) had moved to Leontopolis, where he would complete his reign of 21 years but incorrectly called Iuput II by most authors, the replacement of Piye to the time of Sheshonk III, immediately identifies Iuput 1 with Iuput II.

This also, by the removal of Iny from the Heracleopolitan line, suggests that Rudamun was placed on the throne at Heracleopolis at about 11 years after Sheshonk III was enthroned at Tanis (the latter possibly initially at Busiris). We do not know how long Peftauawybast had been reigning at Heracleopolis when Piye invaded, but up to 2 years, as he is mentioned as HPM year 28 Sheshonk III on Serapeum Stela.

On correlation with Israel, we have (after Thiele), Menahem acc. 752/51 BC

Pekahiah		742-740 BC
Pekah's Samaria accession		740/39 BC - con. Orsorkon II
Hoshea	"	732/31 BC - con. Sheshonk III

This allows placement of Sheshonk 1's attack into Palestine to help his vassal Menahem against Syrian and Transjordan attack in his 21st year, in the early reign of Menahem, ? 749 BC, whereas Tiglath-Pileser III (TP III) received tribute from Menahem in TP III's 3rd year = 742/743 BC, (ARAB 1-772) - (although Shea1978 suggests difficulties with Tiglath-Pileser's records and claims this 740 BC - Menahem's last year), which was Menahem's 8th or 9th year, the 22nd Dynasty monarchs now being Orsorkon 1 probably now in Thebes, and a young Orsorkon II parallel in Tanis.

It also places Orsorkon II contemporary with Menahem, Pekahiah, Pekah and Hoshea, hence the finding of a vase datable here at Samaria with his cartouche, and Sheshonk III contemporary with Pekah and Hoshea, and Sheshonk III was almost certainly King 'So' to whom king Hoshea of Israel appealed to at the time of Shalmaneser.

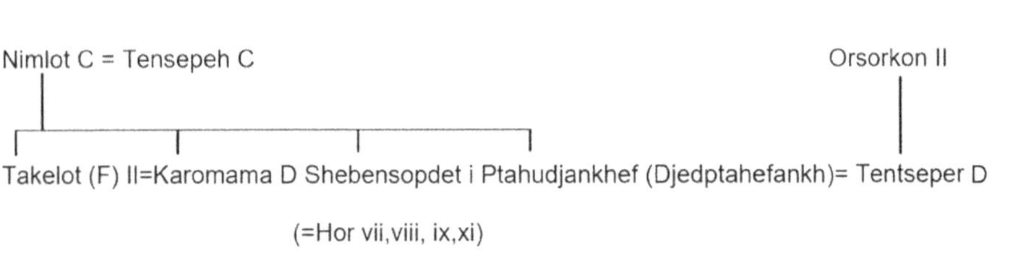

Provisional dates.

Possible reign of Orsorkon II circa. 753 - circa. 710/9 BC ? 44 - 45 years (see later).

" " "	Sheshonk III	"	741 - 689 BC	52 years (son Orsorkon II)
" " "	Takelot II	"	744 - 717 BC	25 years (grandson Orsorkon II)
" " "	Sheshonk IV	"	? 723 - 713 BC	6 (or 10) years. - Heliopolis (son of Sheshonk III)
" " "	Pa-mai	"	689 - 682 BC	HPH Heracleopolis then king 689 BC
	(Pimay)			(son Sheshonk III), (see later)
" " "	Rudamun	"	732 - 712 BC	? 19 years (young son Orsorkon II) Heracleopolis
	Peftjauawybast	?	712- 702 BC	Heracleopolis
" " "	Sheshonk V then		712 - 674 BC	38 years. (son of Pimay, see later) Tanis

Although it must be admitted that although close, exactness here is not guaranteed.

TAKELOT II - grandson of Orsorkon II -25 years
hedjkheperre setepenre netjer heqa waset
radiant one of the manifestations of Ra, chosen by Ra, divine ruler of Thebes
Horus - *Ka nakht kha em Waset* - strong one who appears in Thebes.
Takelot sa Aset meryamun - Takelot son of Isis, beloved of Amun.

Considered first of the 23rd Dynasty.

It is very clear, as Aston has outlined (JEA 75 1989, p. 139-153), that Orsorkon II and his grandson Takelot II, then controlled Thebes, and was dominant there while the latter's uncle Sheshonk III ruled at Tanis (which Orsorkon II also controlled contemporary with Priest-king Psusennes 1).

Takelot appears to have ruled for 25 years (previously recognised as HPA Takelot F), and was succeeded after a gap, a period of conflict (17 years), by Orsorkon III (year 39 of Sheshonk III), who had previously acted as HPA Orsorkon B.

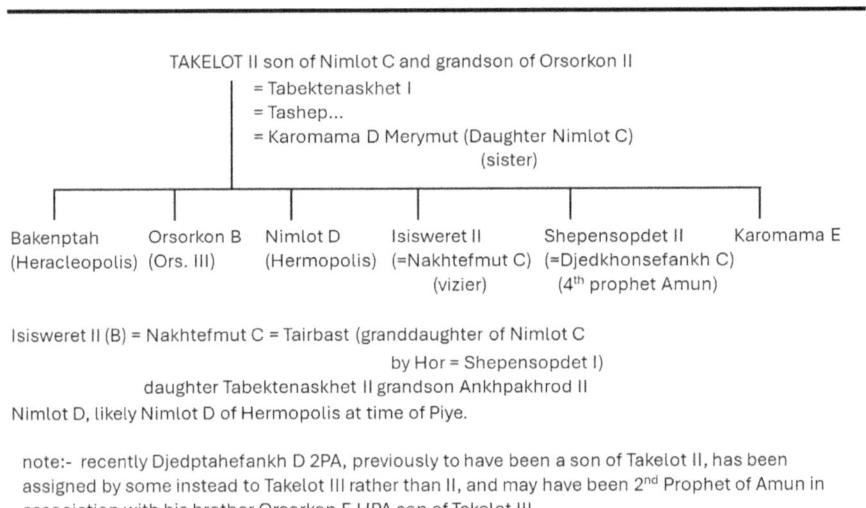

SHESHONK III a son of Orsorkon II

Horus *Ka nakht mesut Ra* - Strong bull offspring of Ra

Usermaatre setepenre Sheshonk (& setepenamun)

Justice of Ra is powerful chosen by Ra, (chosen by Amun)

Shesheneq meryamun, *sa Baset, netjer heqa Iunu*

several variants - but Sheshonk beloved of Amun, son of Bastet, divine ruler of Heliopolis

Per Aa Shesheneq - Pharaoh Sheshonk.

Here equated with "Chief of the Ma, Sheshonk, of Busiris" of the Piankhi Stela.

Father Orsorkon II - "Memorial Stone of satrap Ped-ise and his sons Pef-tat-bast and Takelot." year 28 Sheshonk III. Son Takelot B and therefore C, grandson HPM Pediese.

Sheshonk was appointed in Tanis (possibly first at Busiris) by father Orsorkon II, 3 years after Orsorkon's grandson Takelot II was appointed in Thebes and is said to have reigned 52 years.

Sometime during Sheshonk III's reign he took control of Heliopolis as well, and adopted the title Haq An, - ruler of Heliopolis. I believe this followed the end of the 20th Dynasty, or after Ramses XI's move to Thebes year 19, the last ruler holding that title being Ramses XI. This suggests that the 20th Dynasty (which will be further discussed) expired during the early part of Sheshonk III's reign (although the control may have begun earlier following the move of Ramses XI's move to Thebes). As Sheshonk IV (Hedjkheperre setepenre Sheshonk IV- 6 (or 10) year reign), also held the title Haq An, it is possible that a) he was a son of Sheshonk III, b) was appointed soon after Sheshonk III took that title in co-reigning capacity, dying before his father, and buried later as a secondary burial with Sheshonk III, at Tanis.

Sheshonk V Sheshonk III's grandson also held the title Haq An, although there is no present evidence that his immediate father Pamai (Pamay) held such.

The adoption of this title (Haq An), first by Sheshonk III in the 22nd Dynasty is, I believe an important point of reference, and so would connect the middle of the reign of Sheshonk III with the time of death of Ramses XI (or at the time of the move of Ramses XI to Thebes at the start of *whm wmst* - renaissance period - year 19).

Sheshonk III put his son Bakennefi A, over Heliopolis and Athribis, this would have happened soon after he is first attested at Heliopolis claiming title Haq An and it is likely that Bakenaffi -army leader was contemporary with Sheshonk IV, under Sheshonk III's rule. Bakeneffi was present at the time of Piye's invasion, but no suggestion of Sheshonk IV's presence, suggesting that he died shortly before that event.

We cannot be certain of the year that Sheshonk III took the title Haq An, but after the 20th year is likely, on this revision circa. 721 BC.

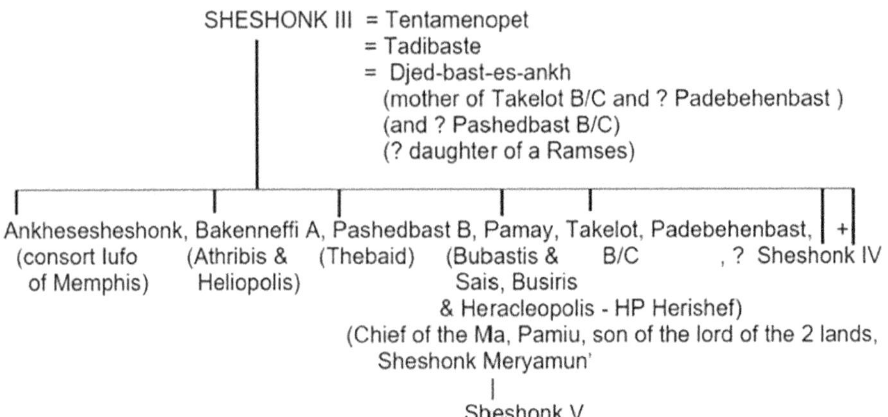

legend:-

Pimai - [Count and Chief of Heracleopol]is, High Priest of Herishef, Lord of Heracleopolis, mek-chief of kahtan Pimai. during the early 20's of Sh III, according to Kitchen- 300, during time of Pedubast I (= y 8 - y 30 Sh III)

Also known from Piankhi Stela "Pamai count chief of the Ma Busiris".

Chief of the Ma, son of the lord of the two lands Pamiu, dedicated statue at Sais.

Padebehenbast - "HP of Amunresonter, Mek-prince of Pawer..., Army- leader, king's son of Ramses" - donation stela year 28 of Sheshonk, HP ? Tanis.

Bakeneffi A "Great Prince, chief of the two lands, Eldest King's son of the lord of the two lands, Army Leader" - stela from near Heliopolis. Heliopolis and Arthribis.

Takelot C - Great chief of the Ma, Son of the lord of the two lands, active at Busiris, -stela year 18 ? Sh III. Almost certainly the same as Takelot B

(mother Died-bast-es-ankh), King's son of Ramses, commander of all troops, great chief of [...]. ('king's son of Ramses' - does this imply one of Sh. III's wives was a daughter of a Ramses ?)

Pashedbast B almost certainly the same as Pashedbast C (Kitchen 93), king's son of Ramses - name found in burial of Orsorkon's son Harnakht together with items pertaining to Amenope (21st Dyn.)

? Ewelhon A - [Great Chief(?) of Pi-] Sekhemkheperre, commander of Tuhir -troops, Army Leader and Prophet of Amun, Lord of Per-Khenu (Cairo JdE 45530)

Sheshonk IV *hedjkheperre setepenre netjer heqa iunu.* Heliopolis

Takelot B HPM, father of Pediese by Tashbastperu (daughter of Orsorkon II). Same person as Takleot C.

Clearly Sheshonk III held power from Sais to Heracleopolis and to Tanis, incorporating Heliopolis during his reign towards the end of Dynasty 20. However, he is apparently not witnessed further south than Heracleopolis. Contemporary with Takelot II, Pedibast I and Orsorkon III, as well as overlapping reign of his father Orsorkon II. He is recognised in Busiris on the Stela of Piankhi, as are his sons Bakeneffi A (and his son Nesnaiu), Pamai, grandson Pediese A and great grandson Peftauawybast. All of this suggests the long reign claimed of 52 years.

THE DAKHLEH STELAE - moments of correspondence.

1) The small Dakhleh stela (Jac J. Janssen 1968, JEA 54. p.165-172), the 24th year of Piye which on this revision would be 708 / 7 BC. Shamin chief Nes-Djehuty (Esdjehuty) mentioned
2) The Large Dakhleh Stele (Gardiner 1933, JEA 19), apparently dated to year 5 of a Sheshonk, concerning a land grant previously granted in year 19 of Psusennes 1 (On this revision that is close to 731 BC). The Sheshonk could be Sheshonk III (Tanis), and the year of the stela then would be circa 736 BC. However, both Sheshonk VI (Thebes) and Sheshonk IV (Heliopolis) are also possible, and both these reigns would be further in time from the 19th year of Psusennes 1, and geographically Sheshonk VI (Thebes 23rd Dyn. 712-707 BC, 5th year would be 706 BC) He would be closer to the Oasis, and possibly then in closer communication, and such would fit the picture better - such would make sense against Takelot II - of the next stela (see below) - both kings relating to Thebes, as would Piye (Piankhi) in his 24th year. My personal conviction is that this Stele refers to Sheshonk VI son of Pedubast 1, reigning in Thebes.
3) Another stela found set up supposedly in year 13 of Takelot III, recently found 2005, also mentions a chief of the Shamin Nes-Djehuty (Esdjehuty), also mentioned in the small Dakhleh Stele. (Olaf and Demaree 2005)

However, with regard to this Stela, the name of the king is "Takelot Si-ese Meryamun" which is also a birth name variant of Takelot II, and I believe that Olaf and Demaree are incorrect in assigning this to Takelot III, as a result of the conventional chronology. The year then would be 731 BC the 13th year of Takelot II, corresponding to the 10th year of Sheshonk III, and the 3rd year of Pedubast 1.

The time between this stela and the Small Stela would be 23-4 years, over which time Chieftain Nes-Djehuty (Esdjehuty) of the Shamin ruled in the Dakhleh Oasis.

The time between the Large Stela and the last mentioned then would be 5 years (if the king is Sheshonk III, but 25 years if Sheshonk VI (the most likely)), is the one, and the land grant in the days of Psusennes 1 mentioned in the large stela would be sometime around 731 BC (exactness is not here possible).

This conclusion negates the last mentioned year of Takelot III (supposed) which has been based solely on the details of this shield, the assumption being that it refers to Takelot III (year 13), so leaving the highest year date of Takelot III as year 7.

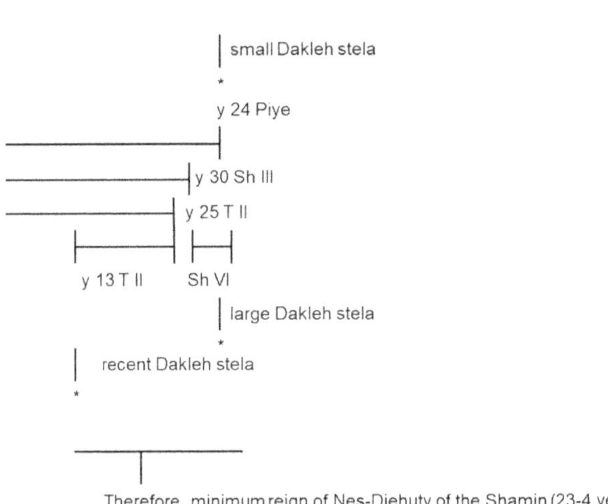

22nd DYNASTY RULERS AT HELIOPOLIS (Haq An)

Sheshonk III - son Bakenneffi A appointed

Then Sheshonk IV most likely dying before 28th year of Sheshonk III

Although no evidence of title Haq An, Pami is attested making a donation in his 7th year to the temple in Heliopolis, but this was likely after he became king at Heracleopolis after the death of Sheshonk III. On this revision it would be dated before 682 BC

Lastly Sheshonk V, Haq An.

These almost certainly following 20th Dynasty - Ramses XI (whose demise I have reasoned to have been circa. 718 - 14 BC), and these followed one another, although it is to be assumed that Sheshonk IV and followed by the early years of rule of Sheshonk V at Heliopolis were contemporary with Sheshonk III Tanis, and no doubt under his ultimate control.

SHESHONK IV- *Hedjekheperre setepenre* Sheshonk IV.
netjer heqa Iunu divine ruler of Heliopolis.
Hedjkhepere meryamun - sibast heqa Iunu - son of Bastet ruler of Iunu.

This recently discovered ruler (Stela Hermitage 5630, Leningrad), is now recognised as ruling, most likely in Heliopolis co-regent with Sheshonk III. He is believed to have reigned for 6 (but likely 10) years.

His burial was found in the Tanite burial site of Sheshonk III, and claimed as a later burial, from a reign later than Sheshonk III (Sh III), but rather it is reckoned to be a secondary burial performed after the death of Sheshonk III. I am inferring that his reign was during Sh, III's own reign but in Heliopolis (hence heqa Iunu), Sh. III in Tanis. His burial with Sheshonk III would add some strength to him being a later son of Sheshonk III, dying before his father to whose tomb his burial was added later. This then suggests that he is a brother of Pimay but dying before Pimay.

I would place him at Heliopolis reigning parallel with Sheshonk III, but before Sheshonk V, who I believe was coregent afterwards with Sheshonk III, at first. And as such I reject the notion that he reigned AFTER Sheshonk III's 39th year. There is no reason to reject the 52 year reign of Sheshonk III, which is calculated from the Apis stelae.

Sheshonk IV is mentioned on the St Petersburg Stele 5630, of Libu Chief Niumataped, the 10th year of Sheshonk IV being mentioned.The same chief has been associated with the 8th year of Sheshonk assumed to be Sheshonk V, but could also just as well be Sheshonk IV,(the title 'Chief of the Libu' also being mentioned during the 31st year of Sheshonk III).On this revision, these three dates would be close to within a 10 year margin of each other, Sheshonk IV dying before the 28th year of Sheshonk III, and Sheshonk V beginning his co-regency close to the 30th year of Sheshonk III. (see later)

On this revised chronology the first mention of 'chief of the Libu' would, in fact, be the 10th year of Shehonk IV, rather than the 31st year of Sheshonk III (although the Wikipaedia list 27th/3 2025 mentions a year 4, 8 and 10 associated with Niumataped and Sheshonk, and such would place 3 consecutive dates before Sheshonk III year 31, and likely associated with Sheshonk IV).

There is naturally a claim that Sheshonk IV reigned after Sheshonk III, whose reign then is claimed to be 39 years. But it seems strange that if a likely son of Sheshonk III, and brother of Pimay reigned AFTER Sheshonk III why his whole existence is so obscure, such is easier to understand if as a brother of Pimay, he reigned and became deceased before him, possibly being older than Pimay and reigning parallel at Heliopolis while Pimay was acting as high priest of Herishef at Heracleopolis. Moreover, if Sheshonk IV was 'Haq An', there is no place for him as such between Sheshonk III and Sheshonk V who also held that title, but such would be easy to understand if Sheshonk IV was placed over Heliopolis under Sheshonk III while the latter held Busiris to Tanis.

PAMI- *Usermaatre setepenre Pami*, variant *setepenamun meryamun*, reign 7 years. (High Priest of Herishef, then King at Heracleopolis - nen-nesut).

PIMAY

Count and chief of the Ma - Pamui of Busiris (Piankhi Stela) -cont. chief of the Ma Sheshonk.

Great chief of the Ma, Pamiu, son of the Lord of the two lands Sheshonk Meryamun Cairo 9430.

High Priest of Heryshef, lord of Heracleopolis, mek-chief of Kahtan Pimai.

Severe confusion resides around this individual. The majority see them as 2 individuals, this author takes the minority view that they are one and the same.

He is identified as the father of Sheshonk V, who followed soon after Sheshonk III.

Pami = "the cat" (suggested from Bastet the cat god), the other name Pimay = 'the lion', son of Sheshonk III.

Pimay is recognised as the third son of Sheshonk III and great chief of the Ma at Bubastis and Sais., during the reign of Sheshonk III. and father of Sheshonk V.

There is a clear association of Pami on Stela with Sheshonk III, from the serapeum at Saqqara.

Pimay, son of Sheshonk III does not seem to have had the title Haq An. This would be so if he ruled at Bubastis and Sais and Busiris, rather than covering Heliopolis. However, Kitchen (300) sites a PIMAI, high priest of Herishef, who was Lord of Heracleopolis (one of the chief towns of the Bubastite 22nd Dynasty), prior to the accession of Hem-Ptah A son of Nimlot C (who also was contemporary with reign of Sheshonk III) and corresponding somewhere in the earlier to middle period of the reign of Sheshonk III. This may well be Pami corresponding then to Pimay son of Sheshonk III. The time fits with the details of both Pami amd Pimay father of Sheshonk V. (Kitchen, p 339-40). If these names are connected, then, despite the paucity of contemporary detail, he was clearly given strong authority under Sheshonk III at the time of Pedubast I, exercising wide jurisdiction, Bubastis and Sais and Herocleopolis and Busiris, with some association with Heliopolis.

Pamai was also mentioned on the Piankhi Stele as count of the Ma in Busiris, on this revision I have placed this year 711 BC and circa. the 30th year of Sheshonk III.

Pamai is later cited in year 2 as king (no longer priest) 26 years after Sheshonk III's 28th year, in association with HPM Harsiese H son of HPM Pediesse (himself associated with the 28th year of Sheshonk III, and mentioned on the Piankhi Stela as hereditary prince), as well, a reused stone block from Heliopolis documents a temple donation from Pami in his 7th year (Tallet et al 1998) - 682 BC on this revision. On this revision his son Sheshonk V would be ruling at Heliopolis at that moment, and circa. in his 29-30th year, while Pami was at Heracleopolis.

Although no absolute evidence is at present known, I am of the opinion that both Pami and Pimay are the same, with difference of title at different stages (the cat—> the lion or vice versa), the son of Sheshonk III (most likely not Sheshonk IV, who I would reason is likely to be his elder brother, on the basis of generation time), covering several different areas under the authority of Sheshonk III, and therefore Sheshonk V is the grandson of Sheshonk III.

There is no known association of Pami / Pimay with Tanis, and his priesthood and later reign (not necessarily immediately following one another) would overlap the reigns of Sheshonk III and early part of V, who were Tanite and Heliopolis kings. It is likely that his major regnal jurisdiction was Heracleopolis and Busiris.

Pimay was buried in Tomb II (reused) in Tanis with other kings of the same period (Orsorkon II, Sheshonk III and IV, and HPA Harnakht). I see him as king at Heracleopolis sometime after Peftauawybast (the latter after Rudamun).

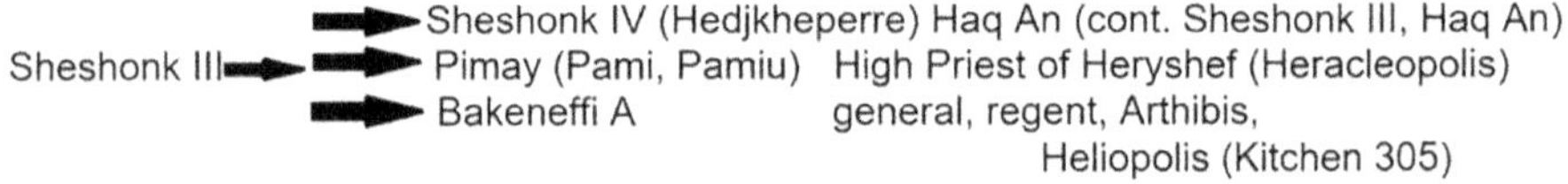

SHESHONK V - *Aa kheperre, Sheshonk meryamun, netjer heqa Iunu.*

beloved of Amun, divine ruler of Heliopolis

This king appears not to have any association with Thebes but recorded in Memphis and the eastern Delta. He clearly was a ruler of Heliopolis, following Sheshonk IV, but it may be that Pami (priest of Herishef, HPH) his father held control before him, as priest at Heracleopolis, but not recorded reigning at Heliopolis, his brother Sheshonk IV being in power there. The next king after Sheshonk V, i.e. Pedubast II and reasonably considered his son was present at Tanis during the invasion of Assurbanipal 664 BC. Petubishti (ARAB II, 771).

His highest year is year 38 on an anonymous stela from Buto issued almost certainly by Tefnakht II of Dynasty 24, the likely father of Necho I (Ryholt 2011) (Perdu 2002). year 36 also mentioned by Tefnakht, and a year 37 by great chief of the Ma-Ankh-hor son of Harbes.

Other chief's contemporary with Sheshonk V- Titaru year 15, and Ker year 19.

PEDUBAST II - *Pedubast sehetehibene.*

Usermaatre setepenamun sa Re Pedubast sa Bastet meryamun.

Almost certainly the Pedubisti mentioned by Assurbanipal at Tanis, he may also be the Pedubast, no. 1 of Manetho's 23rd Dynasty at Tanis. see later.

At this stage we need some comments concerning the Dynasty represented by Pedubast 1, Iuput 1 and Sheshonk VI, (which had come from Harsiese A). This is considered the Alternate 23rd Dynasty but has no relationship with the Tanite 23rd Dynasty of Manetho.

It is recognised that this period involved conflict between the dynasties that started with Takelot II at Thebes and Pedubast 1 at Thebes, involving Pedubast and possibly his sons against Orsorkon B (later Orsorkon III) son of Takelot II. This then being resolved, as far as rule of Thebes was concerned, in year 39 of Sheshonk III.

The parentage of Pedubast has been debated but considering the geography and the known close relationships at the time, it is likely that Pedubast I was a son of Harsiese A (ruler at Thebes, known to have a son—du/'awti and briefly HPA, and therefore a cousin of Orsorkon II). He then was left aside as Takelot II, grandson of Orsorkon II was elevated to kingship at Thebes.

Almost certainly Pedubast would have assumed a right to the Theban throne, especially as he was most likely a son of the previous king Harsiese A.

I believe this is a credible explanation of the beginning of the conflict, but it is conceivable and likely that Pedubast was very young on the death of Harsiese A, and unable to assert his supposed rights for the 11 + years which expired before he finally assumed power.

That conflict appears to have begun in year 11 of Takelot II (= year 8 of Sheshonk III), so that on the death of Takelot II after a 25 year reign. Thebes appears to have been occupied by Pedubast 1, then Iuput 1 (who is believed to have been earlier co-regent with his father).Then 6 years of Sheshonk VI on Pedubast's death, who therefore is reasoned to be son or more likely brother of Iuput 1, and then a 5 year reign of Iny, who may well have been another brother.

So that a hiatus of 17 years before the throne was occupied by Takelot II's son Orsorkon III (previously Orsorkon B in conflict with Pedubast and sons). Such almost certainly involved the rule of residual years of Pedubast, then a period by Iuput 1 then 6 years of Sheshonk VI, then Iny as already mentioned, at Thebes. Aston (1989) speculated that the family of Orsorkon B (later III), retreating to Heracleopolis for 10 years, finally reappearing in Sheshonk III's 39th year (P. 149-50). During that time HPA's were Harsiese B then Takelot E, almost certainly related to Pedubast.

However several difficulties present themselves, and I believe that these are resolved by a realisation that this dynasty also had connections with the north, especially Bubastis, but also Leontopolis in a parallel rule with Sheshonk III of Tanis, Arthibis, Busiris and ongoing connections also with Bubastis.

The result is that close to the days before Piye's invasion, Pedubast, but especially Iuput had moved (or added to) their administration northward, explaining the difficulties:-

Pedubast 1 being *Usermaatre setepenre Pedubast si bast meryamun.*
Usermaatre setepenre *Pedubast si ese meryamun.*

IUPUT I (= II), 12 years co-regent plus lone rule in Thebes, moving to Leontopolis for the balance of his 21 years (assuming the years of co-regency were counted, more if it refers to sole rule), where he is found at the time of Piye's invasion.

Iuput *meryamun*
and *Usermaatre meryamun (re) Iuput sibast*

Pedubast II then is the Pedubast at the time of Assurbanipal's invasion (a position also taken by Kitchen p. 396), and is Pedubast sehetepibenre, son of Sheshonk V, not Pedubast 1 son of Harsiese A, and father of Iuput I and II.

The latter also called Usermaatre setepenamun Pedubast si Bastet meryamun, si-ese. as above)

There is no question that this family (Pedubast 1) had deep connections with Bubastis, despite it's initial association with Thebes.

THE 23RD DYNASTY - A very mixed batch.

There are 3 entities that are referred to as the 23rd Dynasty.
1) The THEBAN 23rd Dynasty

Takelot II ➡ Orsorkon III ➡ Takelot III

2) The THEBAN ALTERNATE 23rd Dynasty

Harsiese A ➡ Pedubast I ➡ Iuput (I & II) contemporary with Sheshonk VI then Iny.

3) Manetho's 23rd Dynasty at TANIS

Pedubast (II) ➡ Orsorkon (IV) ➡ Psammus ➡ Zet.

It is clear that what modern scholars refer to as the 23rd Dynasty is quite different from Manetho's 23rd Dynasty. The difference causing many to doubt Manetho's veracity here, however, I feel this conclusion has been too hasty due to lack of present information, concluded simply from lack of present evidence.

However, labels can be quite arbitrary, and it will be shown that all these entities have strong ties to the Libyan 22nd Dynasty.

It will also be clear that there has been a certain amount of confusion both with Manetho and the modern scholars due much to the similarity of many of the names.

MANETHO'S 23rd DYNASTY

N.B. It is here worth reflecting on Manetho's 23rd Dynasty:-

4 kings of TANIS, which does not tally with the modern interpretation of the 23rd Dynasty. Here I am suggesting that this group begins with Pedubast II.

Manetho begins with Petubates (Africanus) - 40 years Petubastis (Eusebius) then - 25years
Orsorcho (Africanus) - 8 years Orsorthon (Eusebius) - 9 years

Psammus (Africanus) - 10 years Psammus (Eusebius) - 10 years
Zet (Africanus) - 31 years.

Here I have placed Petubast II as the one conquered by Assurbanipal (in Tanis), is it possible then that the following kings followed under vassaldom to the 26th Dynasty at Tanis?

That would satisfy some of the questions surrounding that Dynasty. It is also possible (see later) that Orsorkon here (IV) is the brother of Pedubast II, son of Sheshonk V. However, Manetho's years of reign given to Pedubast should be questioned.

In addition, note the 3rd king of Manetho's 23rd Dynasty, whom he calls by the hellenised name "Psammus". It is then interesting to see that that form of name seems common to the 26th Dynasty, under which I am suggesting this Dynasty ruled, see:-

23rd Psammus			Tanis
26th Psammetichos	-	Psammetichus I	Sais
Psammuthis	-	Psammetichus II	Sais
Psammecherites	-	Psammetichus III	Sais
And also later under 29th Dynasty			
29th Psammuthis	-	Psammuthis	Mendes

This then fits with the name type present at that period. Although we have no 'on ground' confirmation of that king. Nor any known details of a king 'Zet', who remains a mystery.

The above discussion of Manetho's 23rd Dynasty is not new as Aston (1989 p.140) has reminded us that K.H.Priese (1970) and A Leahy (1989) have made the same suggestion - that that dynasty starts with Pedubast II then Orsorkon IV.

ORSORKON IV

(*Usermaatre Orsorkon)*, - but formerly called Akheperrre Setepenamun Orsorkon meryamun - Kitchen p. 117) reign 664 - 649 BC. 15 years. Mother Tadubast III.

Considered the son of Pedubast II (of Tanis), his reign most likely followed after the attack by Assurbanipal. Pedibast II here reasoned to be the 'Pedubishti of Sa'nu' mentioned by Assurbanipal (ARAB 2-771), Orsorkon most likely submitted to Psamtik 1.

However, while Orsorkon IV is *considered* to be son of Pedubast II due to his apparent position, a case can be made that he may be a brother of Pedubast II and hence a son of Sheshonk V, taking the throne on death of Pedubast II (? at hands of Assurbanipal).

This then makes him a candidate for the Orsorkon who married Maatkare B, daughter of Psusennes II and father of Sheshonk HPA of Karnak Nile -statue BM 8. And curiously makes a possible case for Sheshonk IIc as brother of Maatkare B. The genealogy would be:-

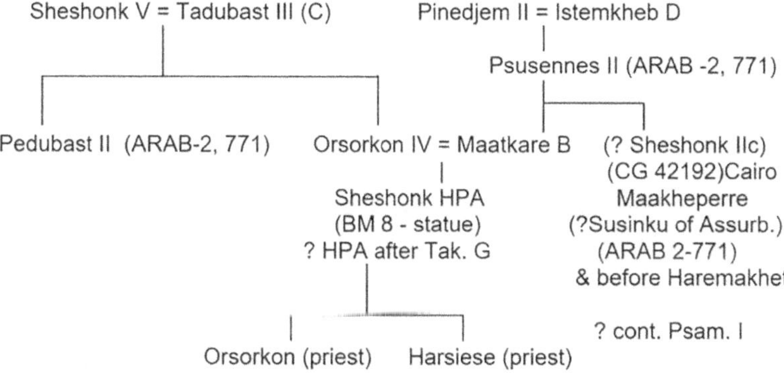

These people initially in place before the conquest of Assurbanipal.

Here I am strongly suggesting Pedubast is the Pedubisti of Sa'nu in Assurbanipal's list as well as Psusennes II (Pase bakhaennuit) as one of the Bukkunanni pi's of that list, NOT to be identified as Bakeneffi D as per Kitchen.

Orsorkon IV then may be the Orsorcho / Orsorthon of MANETHO"S 23rd Dynasty (2nd king)

*

---

note:- HPA Sheshonk (above) consorts 1) Nesitaudjatakhet mother of priest Orsorkon, 2) Nesitanebtashru B mother of priest Harsiese, (Bes Statue formerly in the Alnwick collection), ? contemporary with Psamtek I.

Of interest also is the fact that Pinudjem II had a daughter Nesitanebtashru who is regarded as separate from wife of HPA Sheshonk son of Psusennes II and Maatkare, also called Nesitanebtashru.

With this revised chronology however there is a closeness in time, allowing the possibility that the two Nesitanebtashru's are in fact one, however chronological data would suggest that there are in fact two:-

Nesitanenebtashru - daughter of Pinudjem II and Neskhons - may well be the person in tomb DB320, and HPA Sheshonk - son of Orsorkon (here IV) and Maatkare - married a second Nesitanenebtashru, as well as a Nesitaudjatakhet.

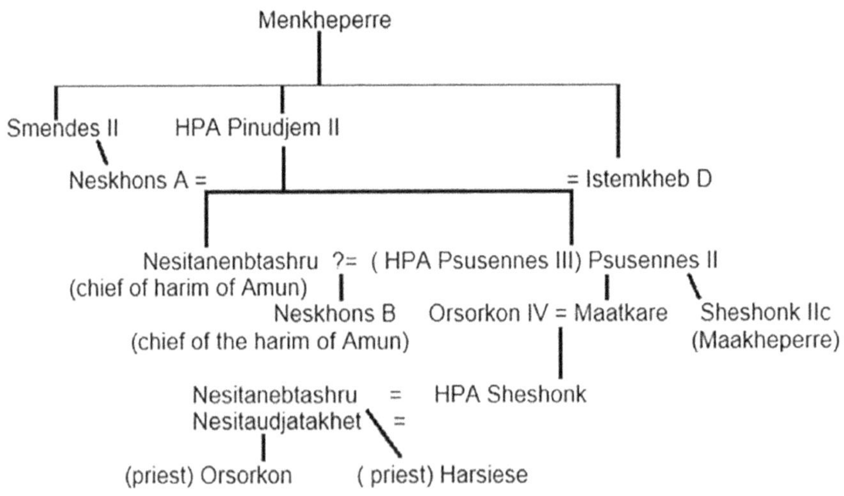

As a result of 2 & 3 PA Djedptahefankh (king's son of Rameses) being found beside Nesitanebtashru in the Royal Cache (the same including Istemkheb D and

Nesikhons, Pinudjem II), it has been ASSUMED that she was his wife, but that is not documented and is unlikely, whereas Sheshonk HPA is documented with such a wife. The parentage of THIS Djedptahefankh is unknown, but he is dated to the time of Sheshonk I and Iuput A HPA, and as such is the earliest body in that room of cache DB 320

THEBAN 23rd DYNASTY

Takelot II, Orsorkon III, Takelot III.

TAKELOT II - has been dealt with above.
His son Orsorkon B became Orsorkon III.

ORSORKON III - 28 years (considered 23rd Dynasty)
Horus - *ka nakht kha em Waset* (strong one who appears in Thebes)
Nebty - *Set ib tawy* (favourite of the 2 lands)
Golden Horus - *mes netjeru* (born of the gods)
Usermaatre setepenamun Orsorkon si-ese
Orsorkon si Aset meryamun

Son of Takelot II, first seen as priest Orsorkon B eventually reigning in year 39 of Sheshonk III, in Thebes as Orsorkon III.

Reign 28 years
(married to) = ? [...]hent-ese (mother Harsiese E)
Karoadjet = ORSORKON III = Tentsai
|
Shepenupet I Takelot III (HPA Takelot G)(of Herishef, first - Kitchen 313 -314, Heracleopolis), chief of Pi-Sekhemkheppere, general and army leader)
Shepenupet I
(adopted Kashta's daughter Amerirdis 1-? 711 BC)
(alive during Shebitko's reign- 707-5 BC)

Robert Porter (private communication) has suggested that Orsorkon III was the Orsorkon who married Maatkare B (daughter of Psusennes II), and father of

Sheshonk HPA of the statue BM 8 (British Museum), that could well be a possibility, but in my view Orsorkon IV would fit more comfortably.

We are also aware of a Sheshonk VIa, also referred to as Sheshonk VII, (a *Hedjkheperre si-ese meryamun* - and hence associated with Thebes), and appears to belong to this late period

We also have to factor in a Sheshonk (Susinku) mentioned, relating to that time, in the list of Assurbanipal (and may be Sheshonk Makheperre IIc), who could be significant in this identification, all at this time, however, needs confirmation.

Sheshonk HPA of the Statue BM 8 may well follow Takelot G HPA son of the lady Tentsai (the later Takelot III), and before Haremakhet son of Shabaka.

TAKELOT III (also 23rd Dynasty)- formerly Takelot G -HPA, Thebes - 5 years co-regent, then claimed to have reigned a total of 13 years, which I have suggested counted the 5 years co-regency. However, the year 13 is from the newest Dakleh shield and may instead belong to Takelot II, and as the claim of 13 years is based on that stela he may not have reigned that long, the earlier figure was 7 years and thus is the highest affirmed. On this revision this would place his 7th year close to, possibly the year before the first attack of Esarhaddon, and raises the question as to whether he survived that. If not, he would have been replaced by Montemhat A (mayor of Thebes), for whom we do not have a starting date. However, I will raise the possibility that Takelot's reign may have been followed by the newly discovered Sheshonk VIa (Si-ese) - *Hedjkheperre setepenre [...] meryamun sa Aset* - (also called VII), who is known to have a year 5.

Continuing TAKELOT III

Horus, Nebty and Golden Horus - *Wadjtawy* (the sturdy one of the 2 lands)

Throne - *Usermaatre*

Birth name - *Takelot si-Aset meryamun (netjer heqa Waset)*

son of Isis beloved of Amun, divine ruler of Thebes.

believed to have reigned ? 13 years, as well as 5 years (? included) with his father Orsorkon III, but as discussed above, the highest definitely confirmed is 7 years. The recent Dakleh shield claimed to be time of Takelot III is almost certainly Takelot II - so that year 13 is not Takelot III.

Married to a king's daughter - Irtiubast, as well as Kakat and Betjet.

Known children:-|

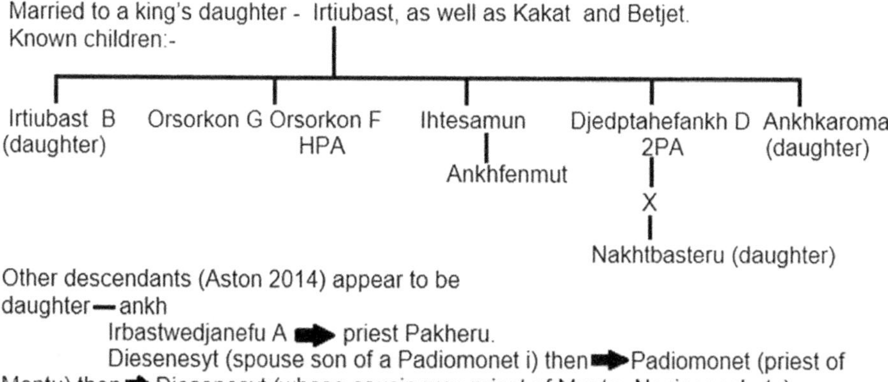

HPA's Orsorkon F HPA ? before Sheshonk HPA son of Maatkare and Orsorkon

Thus HPA's:- Orsorkon F, Sheshonk HPA son of Maatkare, Haremakhet (son of Shabaka), Harkhebi.

The Theban rule of Takelot II, followed by Orsorkon III then Takelot III is recognised as the Theban 23rd Dynasty, however, as mentioned it was not isolated, for in year 11 of Takelot II, a rival administration appeared, and civil war of some degree was evident.

This alternate administration was begun by Pedubast 1, whose parentage is uncertain, but as I have suggested, he is a descendant of King Harsiese A (son), now determined to take back the throne at Thebes.

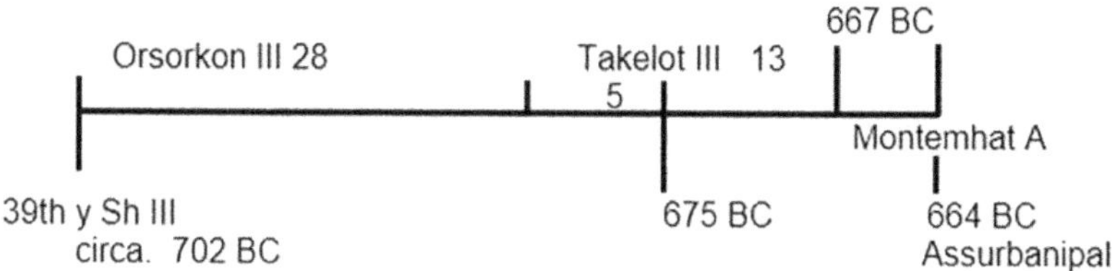

SUMMARY- of the ALTERNATE THEBAN 23rd DYNASTY

Harsiese A, Pedubast I, Iuput (I & II), Sheshonk VI, Iny.

HARSIESE A

HORUS - *ka nakht kha em waset* waset - strong bull who appears in Thebes.
hedjkheperre setepenamun Harsiese
Hor sa Aset - Horus son of Isis

King in Thebes during 1st decade of Orsorkon II, and I have suggested was a son of Smendes III HPA (son of Orsorkon I), the Bes Statue in Durham Museum has Harsiese A claiming his father was HPA (Jacquet Gordon Bibliotheca Orientalis 32 p 358 -360), as alluded to earlier by Aston (2009,p.17) and that was very likely Smendes III HPA, son of Orsorkon I, his sister Tenetamun daughter of a Smendes - chief of the Harim of Herishef.

Harsiese A's daughter Istweret I (sister of Pedubast I) married Harsiese C (great-grandson of Iuput A HPA, son of Sheshonk I), who was 2nd then 4th prophet of Amun during reign of Orsorkon II. Which may give some strength to the family relationship of Iuput HPA, whose own daughter Neskhonspakhered married 4th prophet of Amun (4PA) Djedkhonsefankh A, father of Djedthutefankh B (Nakhtefmut A, 4PA), father of Harsiesse C

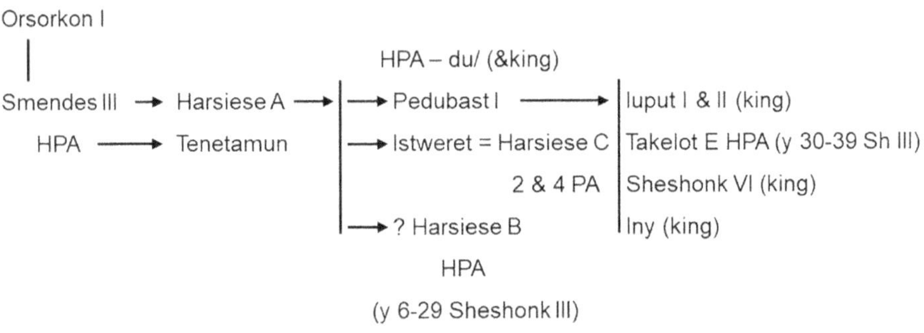

PEDUBAST I

Usermaatre setepenamun Pedubast meryamun, si Ese
Pedubast si Bastet meryamun

Appeared in the11th year of Takelot II - in Thebes, (8th year of Sheshonk III in Tanis), in conflict with Orsorkon B (later Orsorkon III) and Bakenptah, ruling in Thebes intermittently for 23 years. He was associated with possible son and co-regent Iuput 1, who then most likely moved to Leontopolis where he was recognised during the attack by Kushite Piye.

Pedubast was then followed by son Sheshonk VI (formerly known as Sheshonk IV-Kitchen), who appears to have reigned for 6 years, his highest year date known is year 6. But 10 years after Pedubast's reign, Orsorkon III took back the throne of Thebes.

It may be reasoned that Pedubast I was first HPA under Harsiese A *..du/'awti,* then his jurisdiction was usurped by Orsorkon II's placement of Nimlot C followed by Takelot F - HPA (or vice versa) The latter then placed on the Theban throne as Takelot II, Pedubast perhaps being a minor at that time.

Pedubast then took measures to regain his right in the 11th year of Takelot II, ruling for 23 years.

He had a son Iuput I(who I have claimed is also Iuput II), who co-reigned from Pedubast's 15th year, then moving to Leontopolis.

Iuput was then followed in Thebes by Sheshonk VI - 6 years, who was also likely a son of Pedubast, followed for 4 years by Iny, whom I believe was also a son of Pedubast I.

Two other likely sons also need mention a) Harsiesse B as HPA in opposition to Orsorkon B, until Pedubast's 23rd year, then followed by b) Takelot E from Pedubasts 23rd year until end of rule of Iny when he was replaced by the usurpation of Orsorkon III (formerly Orsorkon B - HPA) with Orsorkon's son Takelot G - HPA (the later Takelot III), although Harsiese E [son of x and Ta-]hent-ese, may briefly have been HPA (Kitchen 300 n.539) prior to Takelot G (Kitchen 300).

IUPUT I (most likely also II)
IUPUT I - *Iuput meryamun*
IUPUT II - *usermaatre setepenre (var.setepenamun) Iuput meryamun si Bast..*
consort Tent-kat[...]

Appears to be a son of Pedubast I, at first co-regent starting y 15 of Pedubast (hence 8 years), then moving to Leontopolis, leaving possible brother Sheshonk VI at Thebes. He is known to have a year date - year 21 (which is assumed to be his sole reign).

Iuput I early co-regent with Pedubast 1 (y 15), and contemporary with Sheshonk III (y 23), Iuput II is present at the conquest of Piye, which I date to time of Sheshonk III, the conclusion is that Iuput I and II are the same person, he moving to Leontopolis after his co-regency in Thebes.

SHESHONK VI
Usermaatre Shesheneq meryamun.

Formerly Sheshonk IV (Kitchen), now recognised as Sheshonk VI following Pedubast I and Iuput I, may be another son of Pedubast taking over in Thebes from Iuput I who apparently moved to Leontopolis, the latter reigning contemporary and present there at the time of Piye's invasion.

He is likely the Sheshonk year 5 of the Large Dakleh Stela, his place of reign being Thebes and closer to the Oasis than either Sheshonk III or Sheshonk IV.

Sheshonk VI attested Nile Quay Text no. 25, and roof of Temple of Montu at Karnak. As well as on the statue of Hor IX CG 42226, who apparently died under his reign.

(Hor IX, same as VII, VIII and XI, can be connected with Orsorkon II, Pedubast I, and Sheshonk VI, and such demands that Orsorkon II may have lived beyond Sheshonk III's 31st year)

INY
Si-Ese meryamun

The details of this king suggest that he was in fact a ruler of Thebes, not Heracleopolis as suggested by Aston, and as a ruler of the alternate 23rd Dynasty. I would place him ruling into his 5th year after ? brother Sheshonk VI and then being removed from the throne by Orsorkon (B) III in the 39th year of Sheshonk III.

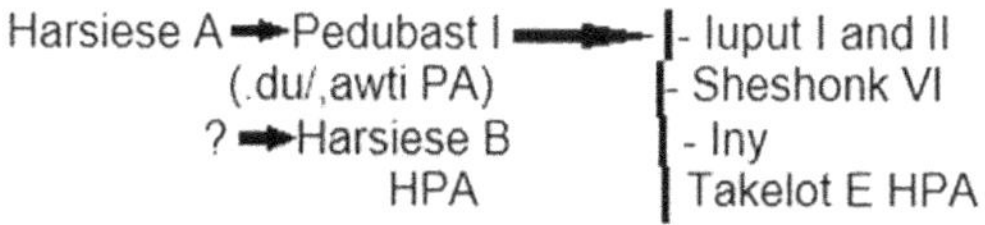

N.B As Harsiese B was in offfice in year 6 of Sheshonk III (2 years before Pedubast's reign - Kitchen -107) through to year 22 of Pedubast I (= year 30 Sheshonk III) replaced by Takelot E the next year, and so it may be that Harsiese B was brother of Pedubast rather than a son.

Year 39 Sheshonk III - induction of a Harsiese (E) Vizier, and "shrine of Amun" (Kitchen - 300 n. 259), no doubt before Takelot G

CAUSE OF CONFLICT IN 23rd DYNASTY.

The conflict that appears to have developed among the 23rd Dynasty was between the descendants of two cousins - Orsorkon II and Harsiese A and appears to have arisen from the ambition of Orsorkon II in particular.

Harsiese A son of Smendes III HPA was ruling as king in Thebes, meanwhile Orsorkon II son of Takelot I (brother of Smendes III) had already placed son Sheshonk D as High Priest in Memphis, and son Nimlot C as High Priest of Heryshef in Heracleopolis (Dyn, 22's place of origin), and Hornakht as HPA in Tanis.

It appears that Orsorkon took the liberty of placing Takelot F (son of Nimlot C) as HPA in Thebes while Harsiese A was ruling, after Nimlot C who had been placed HPA by Orsorkon II - year 16 perhaps on the death of Smendes III, (previously he was HP Herishef at Heracleopolis).

On the death of Harsiese A, it appears that Orsorkon took the opportunity to elevate son Takelot F to the throne as Takelot II in Thebes.

Soon after this it appears that Harsiese B (possibly a son of Harsiese A) took the position of HPA at Thebes, assuming his right as son of Harsiese A, instead we soon find Takelot II's son Orsorkon B as HPA, and in conflict with Harsiese B.

One can only speculate that Orsorkon was able to do this because of the youth of both Harsiese B and his likely brother (or nephew) Pedubast who was apparently given a priestly position (.du/'awti).

Year 11 of Takelot II Harsiese B apparently took the offensive and elevated Pedubast to kingship as Pedubast I, (we know that Harsiese B himself had been HPA at least from the 9th year of Takelot / 6th year Sheshonk III, and perhaps earlier). Whether Harsiese B had become HPA straight after death of father Harsiese A is not apparent.

Conflict now became evident, and soon after this Orsorkon B son of Takelot II was given the priesthood, no doubt by Takelot II (or Orsorkon II - the apparent kingmaker here). The result was dual priesthoods and dual kingships, and obvious conflict.

Orsorkon B is mentioned first in year 11 of Takelot II (year 8 of Sheshonk III, year 1 of Pedubast I) and until year 29 of Sheshonk III. i.e. from the time of appointment of Pedubast I, and to just around Pedubast's death, but absent between year 1 to year 15 Pedubast.

Harsiese B was mentioned first in year 6 of Sheshonk III, i.e. 2 years before Pedubast came to the throne.

Takelot E would follow then for 10 more years (covering reigns of Sheshonk VI and Iny).

Orsorkon B appears intermittently, as does Harsiese B, years 22-29 of Sheshonk (years 15-22 of Pedubast I -while Iuput was co-regent, but also known earlier), then disappears until year 39 of Sheshonk III when he assumes the throne as Orsorkon III.

DYNASTIES 23 at THEBES

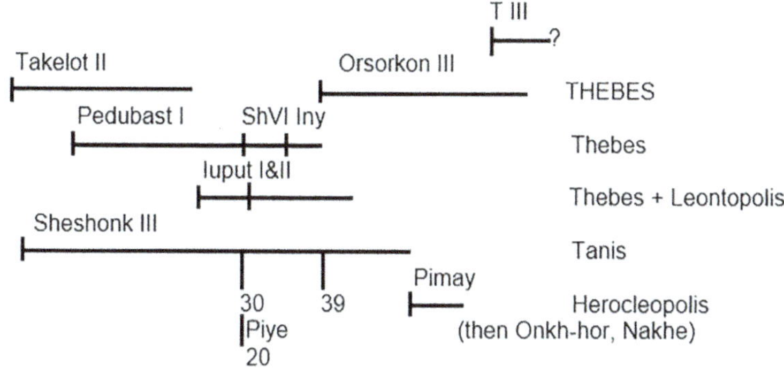

SHESHONK VIa *Hedjkheperre setepenre Sheshonk si ese meryamun.*

Little is known of this king whose name was found at Karnak Nile level 3 (a year 5) - but he has been placed late, and clearly his title associates him with Thebes. (Aston 2009 p.4)

Possibly, but unlikely, for geographic reasons (his association with Thebes -si-ese), one could suggest him as the 'Susinku' mentioned by Assurbanipal for consideration, although this suggestion would compete with the much more likely Sheshonk IIc Maakheperre mentioned earlier).

As Sheshonk VIa is considered late and his title associates him with Thebes, consideration can be given to him following Takelot III, who I have suggested did not reign 13 years but 7, then Sheshonk VIa is known to have a year 5, on his demise we would then place Montemhat A.

N.B. (The Sheshonk on statue CG42192 of Thutmose III, and the inscription from Tel Basta with association of Psusennes II and a Sheshonk, cannot be claimed to be Sheshonk I as claimed by conventional thinking, and is more likely Sheshonk Maakheperre IIc).

THEBAN 23rd and ALTERNATE 23rd Dynasties.

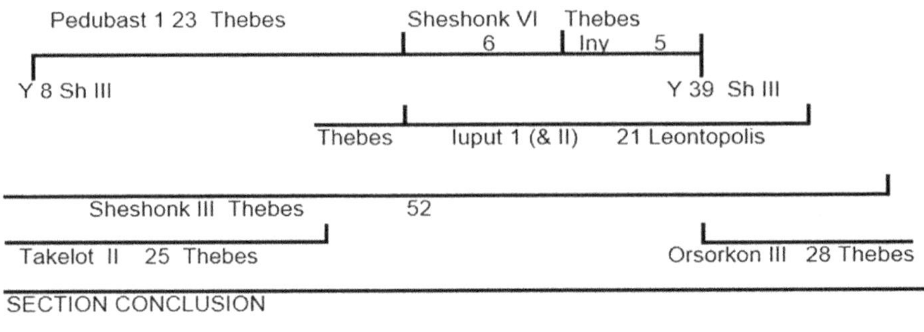

SECTION CONCLUSION

The 22nd Dynasty occupied the whole length of the "Third Intermediate Period" in parallel with the 21st Priestly Dynasty and variously with the 20th to 25th Dynasties.

The beginning can be related to the reign of Sheshonk I but also as will be detailed in following sections also at the beginning of the 20th Rameside Dynasty at Heliopolis, which is not usually included in the conventional linear chronology of that period, as well as the Theban offshoot of the terminal 19th Dynasty. The total period approximates circa. 110 years in total, and not the nearly 500 years placed on it by linear addition.

The period began surprisingly against the background of the last 30 years of Ramses II, whose main activity was in Memphis and Pi-Ramses, it was interrupted after the end of Dynasty 19 in 711 BC by the invasion of Kushite Piankhi (Piye), and terminated largely by the attack in 664 BC by Assyrian Assurbanipal, with the possible exception of several of the kings of the Manetho's 23rd Dynasty at Tanis, who may have continued as vassals under the 26th Dynasty.

REFERENCES

Aston David 2009 Takelot II a King of the Heracleopolitan / Theban Dynasty revisited, The Chronology of the 22nd and 23rd Dynasties (p. 1-28) (p.17).

The Libyan Period in Egypt, Historical and Cultural Studies, 21st - 24th Dynasties Proceedings of a Conference at Leiden University 25-27 October 2007.

1989 Journal of Egyptian Archaeology 75, "Takelot II- A King of the Theban Twenty-third Dynasty" p.139-154.

2014 Royal Burials at Thebes during the First Millennium BC, Cambridge Scholar Publishing.

Blackman, Aylward M. Journal of Egyptian Archaeology Vol. 27, 1941, p. 83-95.

Dodson, Aidan 1993, Journal of Egyptian Archaeology vol. 79, p 267-8, "Psusennes II and Sheshonk 1".

Gardiner, Sir Alan 1933 Journal of Egyptian Archaeology vol. 19.

Herodotus The Histories, Book 4 p. 306 Penguin Classics 1954 Great Britain.

Jacquet-Gordon Helen K. Journal of Egyptian Archaeology 46. 1960, p. 12-23, 'The Philadelphia Statue of Orsorkon II'.
Journal of Egyptian Archaeology 53 (1967) p. 63.

Janssen, Jac, J 1968 Journal of Egyptian Archaeology 54, p. 165-172.

Kaper O.F., Demarée R. 2005 A Donation Stela in the Name of Takelot III from Amheida, Dakhleh Oasis. Jaarbericht van Het Vooraziatisch Genootschap Ex Oriente Lux 39:p 19-37
Universateit Leiden The Netherlands.

Kitchen Kenneth The Third Intermediate Period in Egypt, 1986, second edition Aris & Phillips Ltd. Warminster England

Legrain Georges. 1905 Les recentes decouvertes de Karnak.

Montet J. P. M. 1928, "Byblos e l'Egypte, quatre Campagnes de Fouilles a Byblos" Ch !V

Morkot, Robert, James, Peter. 2009, 'PEFTJAUAWYBAST,king of Nennesut:Genealogy,Art History,and the Chronology of late Libyan Egypt', Antiguo Oriente.

Perez Die, Carmen, 2007, p. 307 n.21. "The Third Intermediate Period Necropolis at Herakleopolis Magna" The Libyan Period in Egypt:Historical and Cultural Studies into the 21-4 Dynasties. 25-27 Oct. 2007.

Petrie, Sir Flinders, History of Egypt Vol. III. 1905, Methuen & Co. London.

Quibell, James Edward, 1898, The Ramessaeum, B Quaritch London.

Rohl David, 1996, A Test of Time, Century Publications, Appendix A, p. 370-71.

Sagrillo, Troy L. 2007, The Geographic Origin of the 'Bubastite' Dynasty and possible locations for the royal residence and burial place of Sheshonq I. p341-360.
The Libyan period in Egypt, Historical and Cultural Studies into the 21st-24th Dynasties.
Proceeding of a conference at leiden University 25-27th October 2007

Shea, William H. 1978 Journal of Near eastern Studies vol 37 no. 1, p. 43-49, "Menahem and Tiglath-Pileser III.

Tallet et al 1998, Des Annales heliopolitanes delaTroisieme Periode Intermediaire BIFAO 98:31-56.

PART 3

THE 21st DYNASTY AND THE NEXUS OF 20th, 21st, AND 22nd DYNASTIES.

ABSTRACT

This section will outline the 21st Dynasty, which is heavily associated with the Egyptian Priesthoods, particularly of Amun and Ptah. But was also heavily interactive with the Heliopolis 20th Rameside Dynasty. And ran parallel to the 22nd Dynasty.

KEYWORDS

Tanis, Thebes, Priest-kings.

INTRODUCTION

The 21st Dynasty of Priest kings finds it's beginning with certain high priests of Amun These became involved in marriage alliances with the 20th Dynasty.

HIGH PRIESTS OF AMUN AT THE PERIOD - Thebes, precinct - Medinet Habu.

MERYBAST- chief taxing master, overseer of prophets of Hermopolis, chief steward of the lord of the two lands - Ramses III.

RAMESSESNAKHT HPA - son, known year 1 R IV (R = Ramses)(Bierbrier 1975 p.11), year 2 R IX. gone by year 10 R IX. Ramessesnakht is key to the real power of the 21st Dynasty priests, marrying Isis the daughter of Rameses VI.His grandson Pinudjem I would marry the daughter of Rameses XI - DH Henttawy, and be recognised as Kheperkhare Pinudjem I, and giving rise to the Theban priest kings following.

The 21st Dynasty then should be seen, not as rise of the priests and the slide of the kings, but as an amalgamation of the two.

AMENHOTEP HPA - son, Known under R IX y 10, 16 and 17, and y 2 R X.

AMENEMOPET 3PA - son-in-law of Ramessesnakht, and grandson of Bakenkhonsu, and son of 3PA Tjanefer I, recognised under Ramses III and V

THE GENEALOGY CAN BE ARRANGED AS FOLLOWING,- (after Ad Thijs)

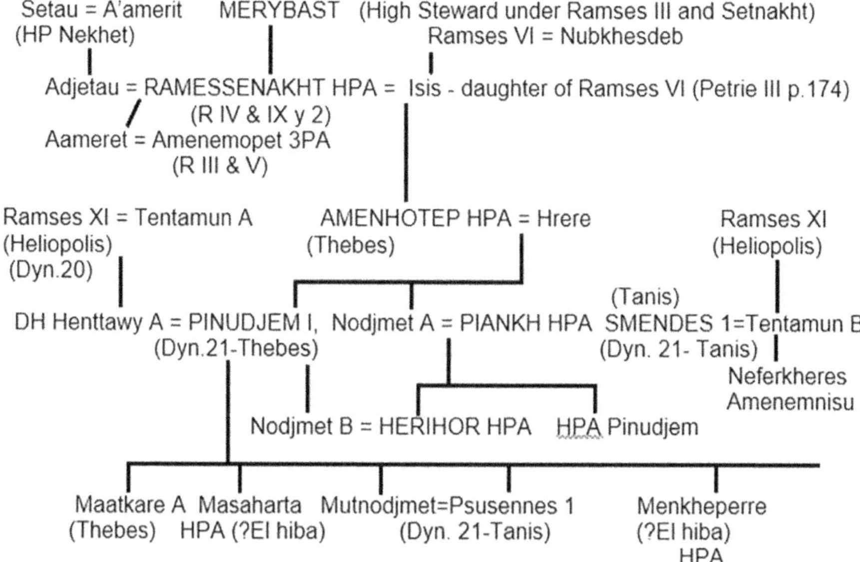

N.B Henttawy is referred to as "mother of the great royal wife" - Petrie III p.204, that 'royal wife' could be Mutnodjmet.

(Coffins of DH Henttawy, Pinudjem I, and Nodjmet A, were very similar, and likely made at same period - Newinski)

At the same time Pinudjem I through wife Istemkheb.

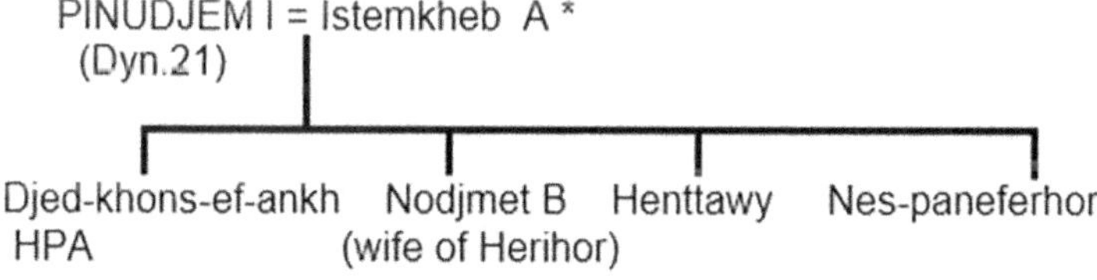

Ad Thijs 2011- in a paper entitled "Introducing the Banishment Stele into the 20th Dynasty" has I believe given a fresh and clearer insight into the events of that period.

Thijs has presented the genealogy concerning the HPA's of that period at Medinet Habu:- (presented with additions from above figure, with numbers for sequential office)

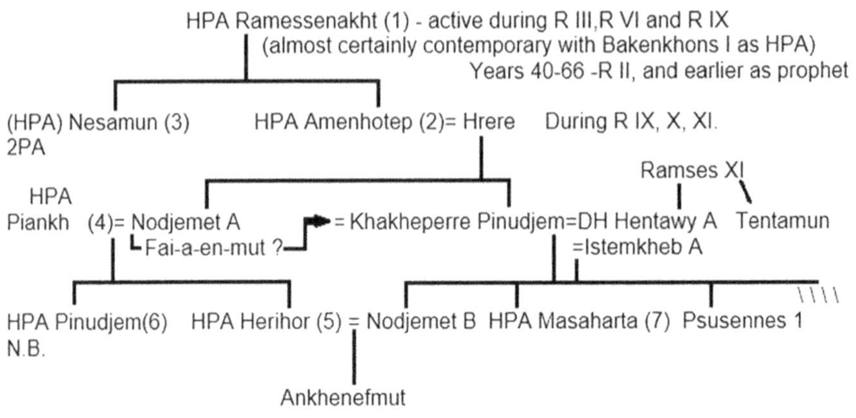

In addition:-

N.B. \\\\ = Mutnodjemet who would be consort to Psusennes I, her brother.

= HPA Menkheperre - stationed somewhere in the north ? El Hibeh or Pi-Sekhemkheperre.

= Maatkare A Mutemhat (GWA), 'god's wife, lady of the two lands' (Cartouche)-(Kitchen p.59 1986)

= Djedkhonsefankh HPA briefly after Masaharta.

Tentamun,daughter of R XI became consort of Smendes I

As well Thijs has made a strong case for the Banishment Stele being related to the 25th year of Psusennes I, rather than Smendes I, as well as making a case for HPA Pinudjem being a separate person and a generation later than king Kheperkhare Pinudjem I. This has given a new perspective to the sequence of HPA's at Thebes:-

There were at least two precincts of Amun at Thebes - Medinet Habu and Karnak, with a possibility also at Luxor, which suggests more than one hierarchy.

KNOWN HPA's at THEBES over the period.

MEDINET HABU - THEBES

1) Ramessesnakht - Time of Ramses III Here will be aligned close to time of Sheshonk I
2) Amenhotep suppressed by Panehsy, who was then driven south by R XI, while Amenhotep ? took refuge in the great Oasis.
3) Briefly filled HPA by brother Nesamun intervention from the north by Menkheperre 25th year Psusennes 1(or Orsorkon II)
4) return of Amenhotep briefly
5) Piankh
6) HPA Herihor son of Piankh.
7) HPA Pinudjem son of Piankh brother of Herihor, at time Herihor became king on death of Kheperkhare Pinudjem I Further HPAs
8) HPA Masaharta brother-in-law of Herihor and son of Pinudjem 1 ? 3 years. 16-18 th year Herihor as king (contemp. with Amenope)
9) HPA Djedkhonsefankh (brief), half brother of Masaharta and Menkheperre. Menkheperre HPA (and king), appears to have been situated at El-Hibah of Pi-Sekhemkheperre rather than Thebes, except for his intervention at the time of the suppression.
10) Smendes II son of Menkheperre HPA (Nesbanedjed), time of Amenope (Kitchen 388)
11) Pinudjem II son of Menkheperre, (under Amenope, Osorchor- 388-389, died y 10 Siamun)
12) Psusennes III son of Pinudjem II, (under Siamun y 10-17, then known as king Psusennes II).
13) Hori son of Nespaneferhor, (installed y 17 Siamun, same year that Psusennes II became king)

KARNAK, THEBES—? the following in different jurisdiction at Thebes - ? Karnak

14) Iuput HPA -time of Sheshonk I
15) Iuwelot - Time of Orsorkon I or more likely Takelot I y 5
16) Smendes III father of Harsiesse A (king) - time of Orsorkon I, or Takelot I y 8 & 14.
17) Then .du/'awti, almost certainly the son of Harsiese A, the later Pedubast I

We here speculate that Nimlot C, son of Orsorkon II previously at Heracleopolis, then became HPA (no. 18) very briefly soon to be followed by Orsorkon's grandson Takelot F (no. 19, the later Takelot II), and very likely placed there by Orsorkon II, and displacing Harsiese A's appointment -.du/'awti, ? Pedubast. This move may well be what precipitated the war between the line of Takelot II and Harsiese A (son Pedubast) - cousins.

? HPA between Takelot F and the 11th year Takelot II, Orsorkon B and rival Harsiese B (combined no.20), suggested by nile level at Karnak -Kitchen Sec 68). Then Takelot E (no.21, likely another son of Pedubast) during reign of Sheshonk VI and reign of Iny Conflict had begun between Pedubast and Orsorkon B/Takelot II

Harsiese B (y 12, the same as y 5 of Pedubast, but previously y 6 of Sheshonk III, disappears after year 29 of Sheshonk III = year 22 of Pedubast I)

Orsorkon B (the later Orsorkon III from y 39 of Sheshonk III, and son of Takelot II - but rival HPA y 11-25 Takelot II, and years 8-39 Sheshonk III)

Takelot E (y 23 Pedubast, y 6 of a Sheshonk -Usermare Meryamun Sheshonk meryamun = Sh VI, this suggests that Takelot E followed directly after Harsiese B, and also covered reign of Iny and was removed by Orsorkon B / III in year 39 of Sheshonk III).

Later:-

22) ? Harsiese E, y 39 Sh III (son of ? Ors. III and [...]hent-ese, Kitchen 300)
23) Takelot G son of Orsorkon III, (later Takelot III for total ? 7, ? 13 years)
24) Orsorkon F son of Tak. III, cont. 2PA Djedptahefankh son of Tak. III
25) ?Sheshonk son of Maatkare (daughter of Psusennes II)

26) Haremakhet (son of Shabako) contemporary with Taharqa and Tantamani
27) Harkhebi son of Haremakhet (y 9 and 14 Psammetichus 1).

Correlation by Thijs
year 25 Psusennes I = year 17or 18 Ramses XI = year—or year 1 of whm mswt.
year 40 Psusennes I = year 32 or 33 of Ramses XI = year 14 or 15 of whm mswt
whm mswt commonly refrred to as 'renaisance period'

RULERS - DYNASTY 21 IN TANIS in accordance to scheme above.

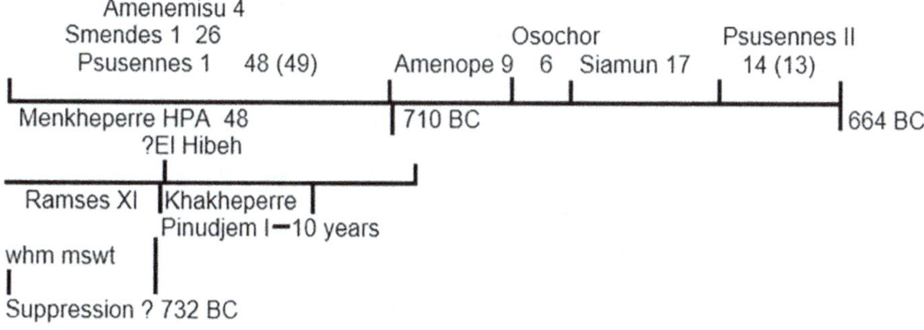

Some difficulties can present themselves here, as Thijs chooses Psusennes I as the king in whose 25th year, Menkheperre intervened at Thebes, 17th or 18th year of Ramses XI's reign, however we do not know how long Menkheperre had been in office.

Psusennes was son of Khakheperre Pinudjem I, and grandson of Ramses XI. This arrangement is possible ONLY if we accept a) An early marriage of Pinudjem I to HD Henttawy, as the daughter of a young Ramses XI. b) then accession to the throne of Psusennes I as a quite young king (he reigned for ? 49 years), and c) the kingship of Kheperkhare Pinudjem I in his old age, d) followed by the 20-21 years of Herihor as king in his old age. Herihor having already stayed aside as HPA for the reign of Ramses XI son-in-law Kheperkhare Pinudjem I, and accession on the latter's death. Year 16 of Herihor (as king), Masaharta becomes HPA.

However, Orsorkon II was largely contemporary with Psusennes I, and buried before the latter's death (Rohl) - so following:-

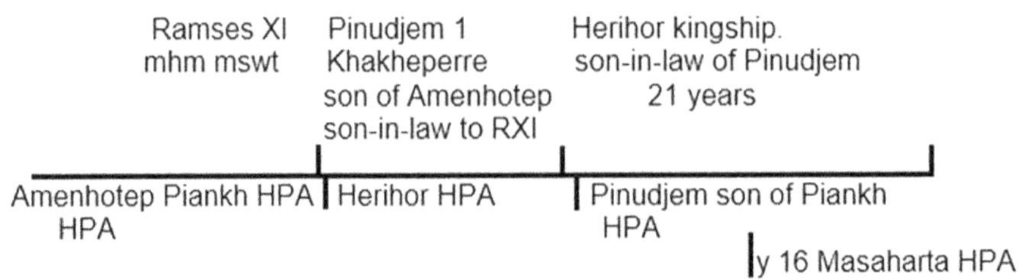

If we accept Thijs' claim that Psusennes I was in assistance with Menkheperre, and that the 25th year was that of Psusennes, and accept that Psusennes handed over to Amenemope at the end of his 48th year. We then can attempt a date, by counting backwards from the conquest of Assurbanipal.

Psusennes II appears to be one of the 2 of that name at the time of Assurbanipal 664 BC (ARAB 2, 771 - Bukkananni'pi, i.e Pase - Bakhaenniut), and counting back this brings Psusennes I handover to Amenope to 712 BC. But with the way Egyptians counted their reigns, this figure can be reduced a maximum of 3 years, bringing the figure to 709 BC (Piye did not reach Tanis- city of Psusennes).Such allows the death of Orsorkon II just before this as David Rohl has claimed (perhaps 710 BC), yet still be the Orsorkon recognised by Piye at Bubastis 711 BC, and the S(h)ilkhanni of Sargon 716 BC, 5 year earlier.

This then allows Psusennes 25th year to be reckoned circa. 733 / 2 BC, also the 17th year of Ramses XI, (who will then have died 16-17 years later 718-715 BC exactness would be difficult).

The whm mswt (renaisance period installed by Ramses XI) then was 733 / 730 - 718 / 715 BC.

So, the 20th Dynasty would have expired 6-7 years before Piye's invasion.

The dates of Smendes I' reign - his 15th year corresponded with death of Ramses XI /accession of Pinudjem I Khakheperre, so his 26 years would end after Ramses XI's death of 718-715 BC (see further discussion - likely 10-11 years later).

Khepekhare Pinudjem's reign (at old age) 715 - 705 or 718 - 708 BC, Herihor's kingship 705 - 684 or 708 - 687 BC.

We can reason that Orsorkon II may then have reigned for a possible 44 + years as suggested by Aston.

SMENDES I *Hedjkheperre setepenre, Nesubanebdjed.* reign 26 years

Married to Tentanum B daughter of Ramses XI

His origin is unknown however some suggestions may be in order:-

His name means "lord of Mendes, the Ram", and until his marriage to Tentanum B daughter of Ramses XI, it is possible that he was "Chief of the Ma of Mendes", forming an alliance with Ramses XI at Heliopolis resulting in his seat as well including Tanis.

On the revised chronology put forward here, he would have ruled during the early years of Sheshonk III, prior to Piye's invasion. We know of a "chief of the Ma at Mendes" during Piye's invasion - Djedamunefankh - dated y 30 Sheshonk III, and a Smendes "Chief of the Ma at Mendes" - year 21 Iuput (I & II), equated with year 42 Sheshonk III, the latter was son of a Harnakht A year 22 Sheshonk III, he himself was successor of Neskhebit year unknown.

Smendes rule appears on the surface to be the result of his alliance with Ramses XI, and not with any known primary relationship with the Theban Priesthood, as suggested here it would have been a strategic relationship engineered by Ramses XI.

The details available suggest Smendes I came to the throne y 19 of Ramses XI which would be the start of the Renaissance Period, *whm mswt,* a moment when Ramses XI moved his activities to Thebes from Heliopolis, an ally in the north would be strategically sensible, particularly a Libyan chieftain. Death of Ramses XI was year 15 of Smendes I, and according to this chronology would have died 10 -11 years after the death of Ramses XI corresponding closely to the death of Kheperkhare Pinudjem I his brother-in-law.

By this revised chronology, soon after the death of Ramses XI (Haq An), Sheshonk III would assume control over Heliopolis somewhere in the mid-twenties of his reign -(Haq An), or slightly earlier when Ramses XI moved to Thebes.

It is unlikely that the people associated with the Theban priesthood during the 20th Dynasty would relate their dates to the years of Smendes I, because he was a northern king/priest.They would date more likely to the Ramesides, the *whm wmst,* or the reign of Herihor as king, all associated with the south at Thebes. The claim of dating against Smendes I is almost certainly incorrect and has been a stumbling-block to correct chronology.

AMENEMNISU *meryamun* *Neferkare heqa waset* - reigned 4 years

This king, who for years has been considered not to exist has been verified by finding a gold cap with his name associated with Psusennes I in his tomb at Tanis.

Several scenarios have been suggested, but the most likely is that he was a son of Smendes I and therefore a cousin of Psusennes I.

Ramses XI = Tentamun A

Pinujem I = DH Hentawy A Tentamun B = Smendes I

Psusennes I Neferkare Heqawaset Amenemnisu

Several facts then become more relevant:-

1) Burial in the same tomb.
2) An apparent co-regent reign in Tanis, where Smendes I also ruled, in some sort of relationship with nephew Psusennes I.
3) 'Heqawaset' (ruler of Thebes) indicating a relationship with Thebes, becomes more significant, despite both their reigns in Tanis, because they were royal descendants of Ramses XI, who had ended with a reign over Thebes.

There is a claim that HPA Menkheperre gave a pardon to rebels during Amenemnisu's reign (perhaps just after the suppression of Amenhotep HPA)

Thijs' chronology has merit, Smendes reign would have overlapped that of Psusennes I, at least until a short time after Ramses XI' s death. This means that Amenemnisu would have reigned a short period in a co-regent capacity beside his father Smendes and during, not before, the reign of Psusennes I.

This may lay behind the confusion created by the Manetho narrative where Amenemnisu (Nephercheres)- Neferkare is placed AFTER Psusennes I while Smendes is placed before.

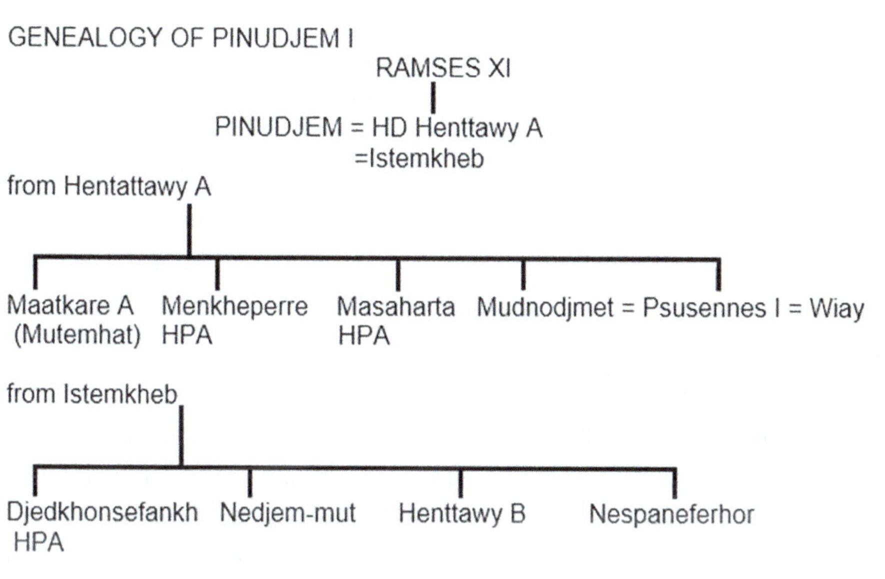

GENEALOGY OF PSUSENNES I

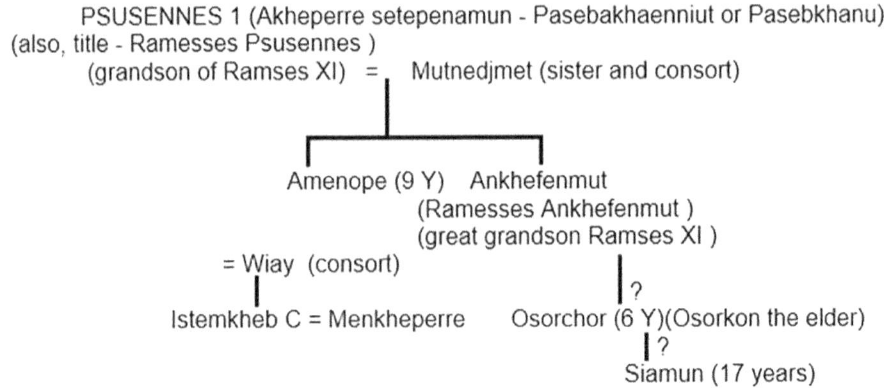

King Amenemisu, most likely son of Smendes I reigned parallel to Psusennes I, 4 years at Tanis.

Psusennes I appears to have reigned for 49 years as a priest king in Tanis, reigning parallel to his brother HPA Menkheperre who appears to have been stationed in El-Hibeh and or Pi-Sekhemkheperre, from whence he headed to Thebes in the 25th year mentioned in the Banishment Stele. Both their burials were in Tanis discovered by Pierre Montet from 1939 and later. However, Psusennes may have handed over power to Amenope after his 48th year.

David Rohl has strongly argued that he also reigned overlapping Orsorkon II (Tanis) who he argues was interred in his tomb before Psusennes I, and therefore likely a closely parallel reign. Aston (1989) has argued that Orsorkon II himself reigned for up to 44 or 45 years, as earlier mentioned, the exact length though is unable to be confirmed.

The "Bad Times" -Ad Thijs 2014 -'The Burial of Psusennes I and "Bad Times "'- of Brooklyn 16. 205

In this article Thijs comes to the conclusion that this document is referring to the short period of rapid deaths of Psusennes I, brother Menkheperre HPA,

Khakheperre Pinudjem I, and another whom he identifies as D H Henttawy. Psusennes I is buried by Menkheperre's son Nesbanedjed / Smendes II HPA, but it is also clear that Smendes I / Nesbanedjed, also died at the same period, but apparently not appreciated by Thijs.

Added to that, Orsorkon II had died just before Psusennes I by Rohl's argument (a Test of Time), and the 25th Dynasty under Piye had just conquered the kingdom, it truly was "bad times" and would seem like Egypt had been changed forever, which indeed it had.

On this revision we would date those events around 710 BC.

AMENOPE *Usermaatre setepenamun, Amenope meryamun*

Son of Psusennes I, died an aged person (no doubt reigning after the long reign of his father), and was buried at San-el-Hagar, he is believed to have reigned 9 years following Psusennes I / Menkheperre, and appears to have been HPA at Tanis before Smendes II HPA then Pinudjem II HPA at Thebes. he would be the Amenophthis of Manetho.

OSOCHOR *Akheperre setepenre* Osorkon the elder, *Orsorkon meryamun*

Little is known of this king and I believe that much of what has been inferred is due to adherence to the conventional chronology.

He may have had a daughter Karimala (King's daughter, King's wife) speculated to be wife of Siamun

A priest - Nespaneferhor son of an Iufenamun- was inaugurated in year 2 (Karnak Priestly Annals lines 1-3, of a king Aakheperre, likely Osochor. And his son Hori in year 17 Siamun.

SIAMUN Horus - *Ka nakht merymaat*
Throne - *netjerkheperre setepenamun*
Birth - *Siamun meryamun* (son of Amun, beloved of Amun)
Highest year date - year 17 (fragment 3B line 3-5 Karnak Priestly Annals)

Pinudjem II HPA son of Menkheperre HPA served early in reign of Amenope, (after brief service of Smendes II / Nesbanedjed), and died year 10 of Siamun., most likely followed by Psusennes III HPA Hori appointed year 17, which suggests that that was his highest year as Psusennes II as king followed Siamun and is believed to be the same person as Psusennes III HPA, (and son of Pinudjem II HPA).

The implication of the last date suggests that Siamun died in his 17th year, Psusennes III HPA took the throne as Psusennes II and at the same time Hori was installed as HPA.

Amenope 9 Osorchor 6 Siamun 17 Psusennes II

Smendes II HPA Pinudjem II HPA HPA y 10, Psusennes III HPA y17 Hori

---

PSUSENNES II *Hor Pasebakhenniut*
Tyetkheperre Psusennes II
Tyetkheperre setepenare Pasebakhenniut meryamun (temple of Abydos)

Psuesennes II appears to have been Psusennes III HPA and assumed the throne on the death of Siamun -year 17, when Hori son of Nespaneferhor was installed as HPA, taking over from Psusennes III.

His length of Reign is considered 14 years but the highest known year is year 13, (line 6, on 3B Karnak priestly Annals) - he may have died in his late 13th year).

He had a daughter Maatkare B married to an Orsorkon believed here to be NOT Orsorkon I but Orsorkon IV, also having a son Sheshonk HPA (who therefore probably followed Hori)

He also had a son Sheshonk (Maakheperre) IIc -(Cairo CG 42192) - who may well be the Susinku mentioned by Assurbanipal (ARAB 2- 771).

In year 11 of Psusennes II, a Nesankhefenmaat (son of a Nesamun) was inaugurated priest, and his son Hor was inaugurated year 3 of an Orsorkon - almost certainly IV.

(Block Karnak 94 CL2149).

We return to Menkheperre son of Khakheperre Pinudjem I and brother of Psusennes I

MENKHEPERRE HPA

He probably ruled mostly at El-hibah and Pi-Sekhemkheperre. The following priesthood were now dominated by his descendants, at Medinet-habu - Thebes.

Uncle of Amenope, but appears to have been active before him. But Amenope would rule at Tanis at same time as Herihor's kingship in Thebes.

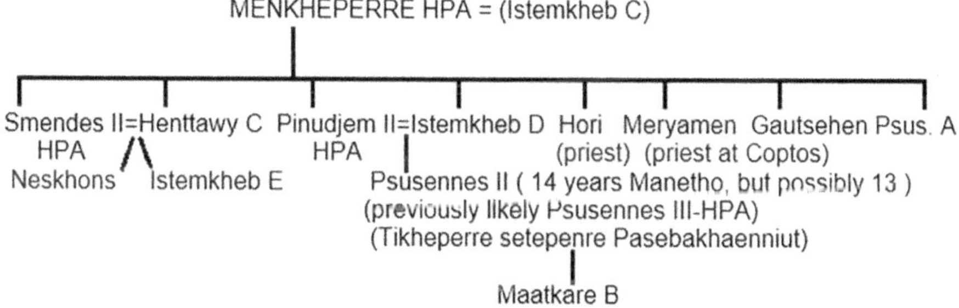

Also :- Merytamun (chanress of Amun), Djedmutesankh

Psusennes A - Pasebkhanut A, priest of Min, Isis and Horus at Coptos and Amun of Thinis

---

Henttawy C named on Karnak pylon years 5,6,8, of a king (most likely Amenope) Smendes II HPA also called Nesbanebdjed (HPA ? 2-3 years under Amenope) married to Henttawy C and Tahent-Thuty.

Gautsehen married Tjanefer A (son of a 4PA Nespaherenmut - Karnak Priestly Annals 3A line 4-6), 4PA year 40 Psusennes I, 3PA under Amenope):-

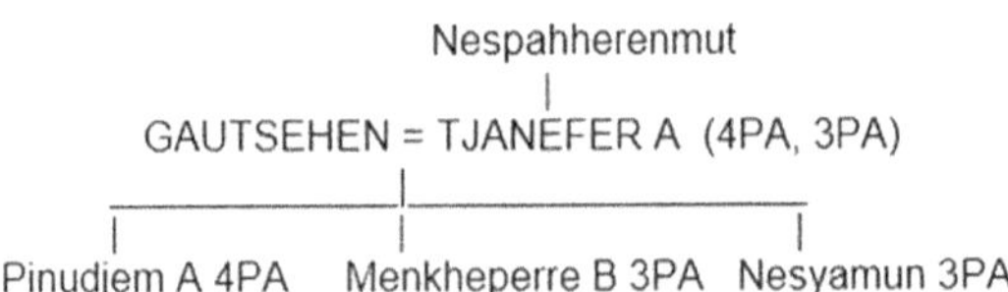

Pinudjem II refers to himself as "descendant of Pasibkhanu" which can only refer to Psusennes I not Psusennes II (his son) -Petrie III p. 209. (via mother Wiay wife of Psusennes I)

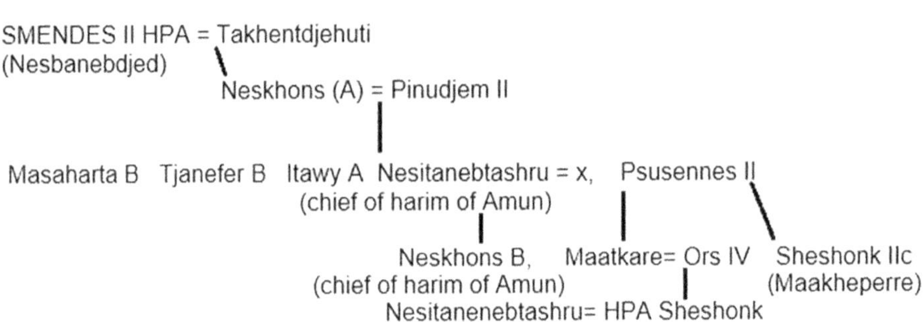

PINUDJEM II HPA = Istemkheb D - descendants - Psusennes II, Harweben, Henttawy D,

Children from = Neskhons - Tjanefer B, Masaharta, Itawy, Nesitanebetashru.)

|—> (Neshkons buried y 5 of Siamun)

Pinudjem II died year 10 Siamun and was followed by son Psusennes II, almost certainly the same as Psuennes III HPA- serving year 10-17 Siamun, then king Psus.II.

HORI - not to be confused with the next person. (details about him seem sparse. Is he in fact a confusion with the next person?) However, his titles appear to be Priest of Amun, Khonsu, Hathor, Sobek, Anubis and Set - apparently not High Priest.

HORI HPA son of Nespaneferhor, installed year 17 Siamun, same year Psusennes III HPA took the throne as Psusennes II. (Nespaneferhor installed y 2 of Osorchor previously grandfather Iufnamun - Karnak Priestly Annals, fragment 3B, lines 1-5.)

TJANEFER A, 3PA, married Gautsehen, sons Pinudjem A, Menkheperre B, Nesyamun.

(Cairo 81, Daressy 151 -Tjanefer Papyrus)

Pinudjem A - 3PA, Menkheperrre B - 3PA, Nesyamun 3PA.

Certain important events:-
Nesikhons died year 5.
Mummies re-interred years 1-10 Siamun. (scribe Butehamun involved)
Pinudjem II HPA
died year 10 Siamun
Hori inducted year 17 Siamun (Priest recorded on Karnak Priestly Annals fragment 3B)

Psusennes III (HPA - son of Pinudjem II) becomes Psusennes II on death of Siamun and was almost certainly Psusennes III HPA years 10-17 Siamun.)

A priestly line found on Block Karnak 94, CL 2149 allows the following:-

Nesamun appointed during reign of Siamun

|

Nesankhefenmaat appointed year 11 Psusennes (almost certainly II)

|

Hor appointed year 3 Orsorkon (almost certainly IV, Dyn. 22 (? Manetho Dyn.23), and after Assurbanipal's invasion 664 BC, the 21st Dynasty now being extinct)

This latter arrangement then throws the length of reign of Psusennes II back to the likely figure of a full 13 years.

ASSURBANIPAL'S CONQUEST 664 BC ARAB 2-771.

The conventional chronology does not recognise any association of the 21st Dynasty with the event of Assyrian Assurbanipal's conquest of Egypt in 664 BC. However, the evidence presented by David Rohl (A Test of Time 1995), identifies a parallelism of the 21st Dynasty with the 22nd Dynasty and so the Assyrians conquest becomes relevant.
This appears to be relevant to the later kings of Dyn.21

KINGS OF THE PERIOD, mentioned by Assurbanipal (ARAB 2-771, 2-844) - 664 BC. Initially set up by Esarhaddon (ARAB -2, 580 and 771)

Niku (Necho 1) king of Memphis and Sais..
Putubishti (Pedubast II) king of Sa'nu (Tanis) 22nd Dyn.
Mantimeanhe (Montemhet A) king (mayor) of Ni (Thebes) - married to a granddaughter of Piye and niece of Taharqa - Wadjrenes.
Bukkunanni'pi (Pase-bakhaenniut - Psusennes II) king of Hathiribi (? Arthibis).
(Pi'bukkunanni)
mistakenly called Bakeneffi D by Kitchen - sect 357)
Bukkunanni'pi (another Pase-bakhaenniut) king of 'Ahni' (? Heliopolis)
(Pi'bukkunanni)
and Assyrian appointee Sharru-lu-darri of Si'nu, (Pelusium)

Other names fitting the era:-
Nakhe king of Hininshi (Heracleopolis)
Harsiaeshu (Harsiese) king of 'Sabnuti'
Susinku (Sheshonk) king of 'Pushiru'. (? Maa-Kheperre Sheshonk IIc son of Psusennes II)

CG 42192

Pishanhuru (? Pasenhor - Kitchen p.397) of 'Nathu" (? Pasenhor B)
Unamunu (?? Wenamun - Kitchen ibid) of 'Nathu"
Tabnahti (?? Tefnakht-Ibid.) of 'Punubu'
Bukurninib (?? Bakenranef - ibid.) of 'Pahnuti'
Lamentu (? Nimlot - Kitchen p. 397) of 'Himuni' (Hermopolis)

We need to recall that Esarhaddon had earlier invaded Egypt 671 BC also during the reign of Taharqa.

If we assume the arrangement of Ad Thijs, for the 21st Dynasty, and identify one of the Bukkunanni'pi's mentioned in the annals of Assurbanipal (above) is in fact Psusennes II, and therefore his reign there terminated, we get the following chronology:-

working backwards
Psusennes II (13) 677 - 664 BC
Siamun (17) 695 - 678 BC
Osochor (6) 701 - 696 BC
Amenope (9) 710 - 702 BC

Psusennes 1 (49) 759 - 710 BC. possibly a couple of years later, due to method of counting reigns and a possibly small overlap with Amenope, so ? 757 - 709 BC.

Assuming year 5 of whm mswt (renaissance period) was the year of Wenamun, then his journey would have begun in Psusennes I's 32nd year ? 728 BC, consistent with my later assessment on other parameters.

A few years shortening is possible, if we take into account that the system was a non-accession system.

Thijs' chronology however, as such, suggests an overlap of Psusennes I and Smendes I, which may in fact be credible with both Pinudjem I and Smendes I being brothers in law, and sons in law to Ramses XI, with Psusennes I (son of Pinudjem) with a long reign coming to the throne in the north at a very young age. In Thijs' chronology, he feels forced to change the position of Wenamun, due to his assumption that his chronology leaves Smendes I several decades earlier, and overlooks the fact that Smendes I was in fact brother-in-law by marriage with Khakheperre Pinudjem I, whom he places reigning parallel to last days of Psusennes I, (this places these brother-in-laws very wide apart), in fact Taylor (1995) made a case for Pinudjem I proclaiming his kingship in the 15th or 16th year of Smendes I.

Of interest is the fact that Bierbrier when discussing the family of scribe Amennakht (p.39) clearly has Smendes at (and late during the time), and after the reign of Ramses XI.

On the contrary, if we can assume that Pinudjem became king late in life, which is not inconsistent with his genealogy and chronology (because Pinudjem was father of Psusennes I), then we can place Wenamun in year 5 of whm mswt (which would be the 5th year of Smendes I, by Taylor's chronology).We can also place Smendes and Tentamun during the early reign of Psusennes I who was after all his nephew by marriage, as well as the later years of Ramses XI -year 19, (see discussion of the family of scribe Amennakht during 20th Dynasty), and leaving Thijs' chronology safe from contradiction in this area.

Then Khakheperre Pinudjem I came to the throne at advanced age after Smendes accession, his brother-in-law had been reigning for 15 years, but Pinudjem had already produced a significant family which would see the dominance of the priesthood at both Tanis and Thebes.

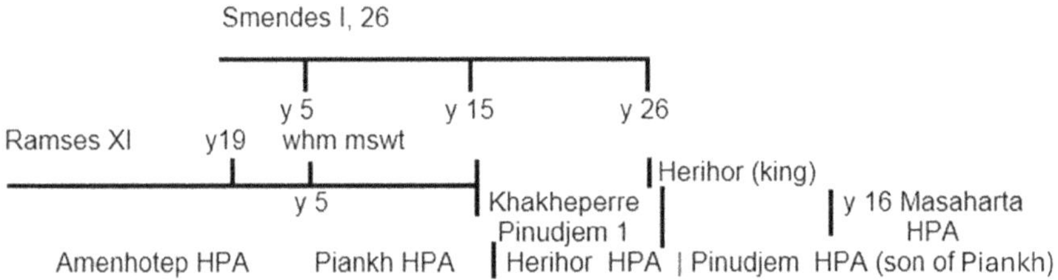

Masaharta HPA has been related to years 16-18 of Smendes I (Kitchen 1986, 383), and probably at El Hiba or Tanis. Concurrent with reign of Pinudjem I and scribe Ankhefenamun son of Butehamun (probably as assistant with Butehamun), however it appears that year 16-18 belong not to Smendes but to Herihor's kingship.

Thijs also has related Masaharta to y 16 King Herihor after HPA Pinudjem HPA son of Piankh, then followed by Djedkhonsefankh HPA briefly.

So would follow Smendes II HPA (Nesbanebdjed) briefly, then Pinudjem II HPA dying year 10 Siamun, Psusennes III HPA (becoming king Psusennes II on death of Siamun), then Hori, inaugurated year 17 Siamun (the latter dying perhaps the next year to be followed by Psusennes II)

THE STATUS OF PINUDJEM I of 21ST DYNASTY

Although the 21st Dynasty is usually suggested to have begun with Smendes who reigned 26 years (married to Tentamun B daughter of Rameses XI), the real thrust behind the 21st Priestly Dynasty came with his brother-in-law Pinudjem I (married to DH Henttawy daughter of Ramses XI), brother-in-law of HPA Piankh married to Nodjemet A.

Smendes I, would produce a son Nephercheres (Neferkare, Amunemnesu), who would reign as a "Tanite" king in Thebes for 4 years contemporary with the Tanite king Psusennes I (Niwinski, 1979).

Pinudjem I, however, would have the following relationships:-

Son-in-law to Ramese XI (20th Dyn.)

Brother-in-law to Smendes I.

Father of Psusennes I (21st Dynasty).

Father of Theban High Priests- Masaharta, Djed-khons-ef-ankh, Menkheperre.

Royal ancestor of both priest - king lines of Tanis and Thebes.

He clearly was the powerful religious force behind 21st Dynasty

Niwininski (1979) emphasised the stature of Pinudjem I.

> *"The role of Pinudjem would become clear. As the son -in -law of Rameses XI, father of the Tanite king and his wife, two high priests and the "God's wife" of Amun, he was without doubt, the central personage in Egypt, of exceptional status. In such a situation, his royal titulary (with only an honorary meaning anyway, as proved by the dockets of*

the 16th year of Smendes and 8th year of Psusennes) is no longer a surprise."

Niwininski, however seemed not to appreciate that Pinudjem I *Kheperkare* was a different person than Pinudjem HPA son of Piankh HPA

During the next generation the balance would swing to the descendants of Orsorkon II, contemporary with Psusennes I, both in Lower Egypt- centres Tanis and Bubastis, and to Orsorkon II's descendants on the throne in Thebes (Karnak) in Upper Egypt. and the contemporaneity of Sheshonk III in Tanis.

Several names here are common to the 19th and 20th Dynasties, the question is whether they are the same people:-

1) Setau- Two Setaus are known, but the evidence suggests two different people.

a) Setau viceroy of Kush wife NefroMut known from years 38 and 44 of Ramses II, buried at Tomb TT289 Theban Necropolis Dra abu el Naga b) Setau High Priest of Nekhbet, wife A'atmerut and daughter Adjedet-aat married to High Priest of Amun Ramsessesnakht, during years of Ramses III, buried at El Kab.

No known relationship is certain, but family connections may well be likely.

2) Panahesy a) Chief treasurer during Ramses II's y 10, 15, 24. b) Panahesy viceroy of Kush years 12 and 17 Ramses XI apparently in conflict with HPA Amenohotep. c) Panahesi, vizier to Merenptah (Petrie III p 106, Stele at Silsileh, Temple Wady Halfa).

On this revision the possibility of the same person is real.

3) Neferronpet, a) Vizier Ramses II year 50, b) Vizier contemporary with Ramessesnakht (R III, IV, V,VI), c) HPM during Ramses II (Berlin 23673, Louvre '96'cat 52), d) HPM Ramses IX, on this revision it is possible though not able to be proven that these are one and the same person.

REFERENCES

ARAB 2, Ancient Records of Assyria and Babylonia, Luckenbill D.D. 1927, Greenwood Press New York.

Aston D.A. Journal of Egyptian Archaeology, 75, 1989, p. 139 -153.

Bierbrier, M L 1975, The Late New Kingdom In Egypt, Aris & Phillips Ltd, Warminster, England.

Kitchen,K.A. 1986, p419 no. 27-9, The Third Intermediate Period in Egypt, Second Edition.

Niwininski Andrzej, 1979 Journal of the American research centre in Egypt Vol. XVI, p.51 & 60

Petrie, Sir Flinders, History of Egypt vol. III. 1905, p. 174. Methuen & Co London.

Rohl, David, "A Test of Time", Century Publications, 1995.

Taylor, H.T., 1995, Procedings of the Seventh International Congress of Egyptologists 3-9th September, p 1148.

Thijs, Ad. 2011, Introducing the Banishment Stele into the 20th Dynasty
ZAS - Zeitschrift fur Agyptishe Sprache und Altertumskiunde 138 p, 163-181 Academia.edu.
2013, ZAS 140, p 54-69, Nodjmet A, Daughter of Amenhotep, Wife of Piankh and mother of Herihor.
2114, The Burial of Psusennes I and the "Bad Times" of P. Brooklyn 16.205.
ZAS - Zeitschrift fur Agyptische Sprache und Altertumskunde 141, p. 209-223. Academia.edu

PART 4

THE ARRANGEMENT OF THE 20TH DYNASTY - A DYNASTY AT HELIOPOLIS

ABSTRACT

This dynasty is not included in the third Intermediate Period under the conventional chronology, but here will be argued is indeed associated with that period.

The case will here be presented that the 20th Dynasty, was a parallel Dynasty, set up during later years of the reign of Ramses II, at Heliopolis, and a duration of a maximum of 50-60 years, those years embodying several parallel reigns and the total period wholly embraced by the reigns of Ramses III and Ramses XI, with the possibility of slight overlap of those two reigns.

KEYWORDS

Setnakht, Ramses III, sons of Ramses III.

INTRODUCTION

The 20th Dynasty is not considered within the 'Third Intermediate Period" in the conventional chronology, due to the interpretation of that dynasty in linear fashion following the end of the 19th -20th Rameside Dynasties. However, the revised chronology here presented argues that the 20th Dynasty is in fact a break-off during the 19th Dynasty and parallel with the early 21st and 22nd Dynasties. Reasons for this will here be presented.

With the revision presented here, Ramses II is dated 792-727 BC (part 1), and the case is made that the 20th Dynasty was a regional administration set up at Heliopolis (with access to Thebes, especially Medinet Habu), particularly to preserve the Rameside brand as the great king was failing and a number of princes had died, whether set up spontaneously or originally appointed by Ramses II, is uncertain, both are possible.

So, a case could also be made that Setnakht, who here is reasoned to be another son of Ramses II (Setnakhtamun- Snechtenamun of Petrie no. 20 and possibly born before R II came to the throne), may in fact have been appointed by Ramses II himself to Heliopolis, as ruler (R II also appointed another son, Prince Mery-Atum - no. 16, High Priest of Re in Heliopolis, ? year 26 -Kitchen 1982, p. 111, 766 BC on this revised chronology)

The founder appears to be Setnakht, father of Ramses III, and most likely co-regent (but possibly for 2 years before Ramses III). He conflicted with a 'Syrian' referred to as 'Arsu' And a likely candidate (though not provable) who could fit is Azariah (Uzziah) of Judah of whom it is said:-

> "... *his name spread abroad even to the entering of Egypt" (2 Chron.26:8.)*, "*...made war with mighty power" (v.13).*

The effective time period in the life of Azariah was 767-751 BC, after which he was debilitated. We have no certainty as to which years such could have occurred, other than the above range of years, but they would fit the likely revised dates for

Setnakht. Soon following this was the rise of the Neo-Assyrian kings under Tiglath-pileser III.(745 BC).

The conventional dates for the 20th Dynasty are 1186-1069 BC (Manley) - nearly 120 years, but this is unlikely. Ramses XI was clearly related by his daughter DH Henttawy with Pinudjem 1 (21st Dyn.), and hence some overlap in their lives. The time period demands a shorter period for the 20th Dynasty, and this can be appreciated by the conditions of the time where family co-regencies were appropriate to hold territorial claims, Ramses III appointing his sons to other towns even while he was reigning, many of whom died quite young.

The main title of the 20th Dynasty kings is "Haq An" - 'rulers of Heliopolis', and only 4 of them held that title viz. Ramses III, Ramses VI, Ramses VII, then Ramses XI (see further discussion for time relationships, below). These almost certainly were not necessarily sequential on death, Ramses III first holding the title, then I will suggest, in sequence, as co-regents Ramses VI, Ramses VII, and perhaps even Ramses XI prior to his sole reign. The other rulers occupying other towns in parallel (including Thebes). This gives a possible reason to reduce the total length of the dynasty, perhaps down as low as 40-45 years, but a maximum of 50 -60. It should also be noted that few of the sons of Ramses III reached significant age, again mitigating somewhat against sequential reigns of these kings. A case for such a reduction will be made following.

Holders of title Haq An. A likely chronological relationship which will be elaborated.

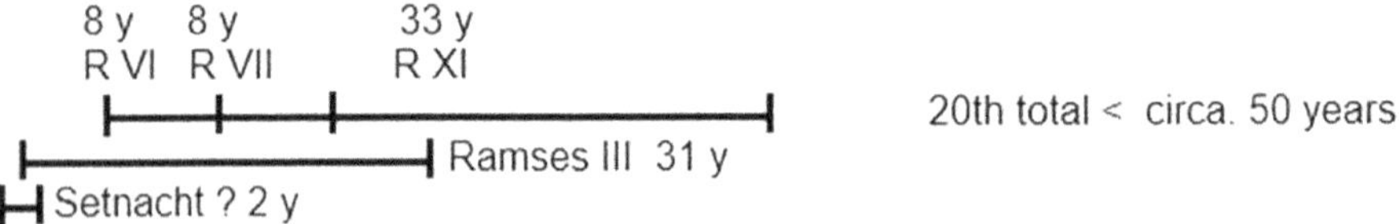

There are some suggestions that R VI may have began to rule a couple of years later than indicated here, after his father R III had been a few years on the throne (possibly 8 years, suggested by the fact that R V was buried by R VI in his 2nd year of reign). But as will be shown there was definitely overlap.

A possible genealogy follows, but some relationships are still subject to debate:-

SETNACHT = Tiyi-Merense   Hemdjert (mother)

RAMSES III = Isis-Ta'Hamadjilat - Pareherwenemef (first born)
(Haq An) *** (great royal wife) - Ramses VI (Amenherkhopshef) = Nubkhesed
(Haq An) *** ── Ramses VII (Haq An) ***
Iset, married to Ramessesnakht HPA
── Amenherkhepshef (died age 15)
── Panebenkemyt
── Pre'herwonmef
? ── Ramses IX

= Tiye
(later executed)
- Khaemwaset (first born)
- Duatentopet (Tentopet - married Ramses IV)
- Pentawere (died 18-20 years old ? executed)
- Meryatum (HP Heliopolis – year 4 Ramses V, Kitchen p. 123)
- Ramses VIII (Setherkhopshef)
- Montuherkhopshef = Takhat (King's mother)
? ── Ramses IX (died circa. 50)
── ? Ramses X
── Montuherkhopshef C
── Nebmaatre

=Tyti
(King's daughter, King's sister)
(King's wife, King's mother)
(god's wife)
- Ramses IV = Tentopet ── Ramses V (throne year 13)
(crown prince year 12, throne year 21)
- ? Ramses X (reign 3 years)
- ? Ramses XI ── Tentamun = Smendes I
(Haq An) *** ── Henttawy = Pinudjem I

Not many of Ramses III children reached any significant age, and this falls in line with the idea of co-regencies rather than sequential reigns.

Known reign lengths:-

Ramses III (R III) - 31 years

Ramses IV (R IV) - 6 years came to throne age 21, then son Ramses V (R V)- 4 years, came to throne age 13 years, buried 2nd year of R VI)

Ramses VI (R VI) - 8 years (lived to about age 40 years), then son Ramses VII (R VII) - 8 years. Both these held the title Haq An, as did R III and R XI. One can therefore assume that they were associated with Heliopolis, but possibly not so for the other sons.

Ramses VIII (R VIII)- 1 year.

Ramses IX (R IX) - 19 years. (he is believed to have died around age 50, during 15th year of R XI)

Ramses X (R X) - 3 years. (dying around 16-17 year of R XI)
Ramses XI (R XI) - 30 (or ? 33) years

How long then was the dynasty ?, Some interesting contemporary details come forward to help us here, related to the workmen of this period. (Bierbrier 1975)

Family of workman Senneddjem. Contemporary work time-periods.

Bierbrier p.30 indicates R III, who earlier is timed with Amenesse, then contemporary with R IV, but also Sethos II and Siptah

following then is a period where only R III and R IV is mentioned

next indicates R IV, R V and R IX in same generational working period.

" indicates R V, R VI, R IX and R X in the same working period.

" then a period when only R VI is mentioned.

then a working period when only R IX is mentioned.

then a working period embracing R IX and R XI.

finally a period embracing R IX, R X and R XI

So R IX who, apart from R III and R XI is the longest reigning, embraces around the reigns of R IV through to R XI, and his reign was only 19 years This suggests parallel reigns, over a significantly short period.

Thus:-

							R XI	R XI
				R X ?				R X
	R IV		R IX	R IX		R IX	R IX	R IX
	Sethos II		R V	R V				
Amen.	Siptah	R IV	R IV	R VI	R VI			
R III	R III	R III						

R IV clearly overlaps R III, and both overlap Sethos II and Siptah.

Again, Bierbrier lists another family of the time p.36, - Family of Kaha (chief workman of the left hand)

1st 'working period' of 20th Dynasty R III, but also Siptah and Amenesse			
2nd	'working	period'	R III and R VI.
3rd	"	"	R III, R IV, and R IX.
4th	"	"	R IX.
5th	"	"	R XI.

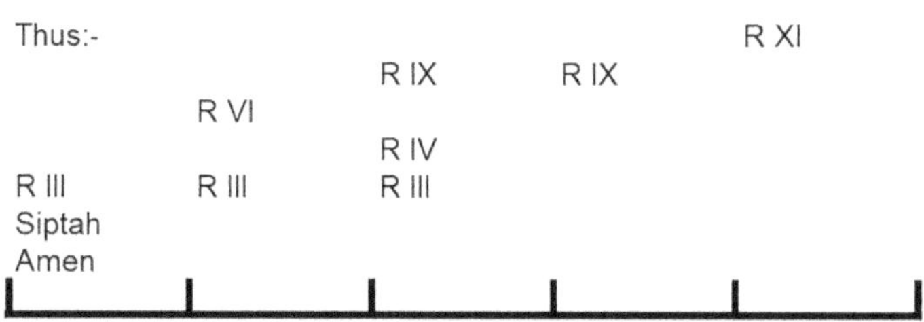

R IV, R VI and R IX all overlap R III.

The family of the scribe and scribes of the Necropolis Amennakht X, a very significant family during the years particularly of R XI. Bierbrier p. 39 -42, Wood 2020.

Significant also is the fact that several of the generations are known to overlap in their functions.

Amennakht X - during R III years 16 and 24, and R VI year 1.

Harshire (Horisheri) -son- years 21,28, 29 of R III, years 3-4 & 6 R IV, y 3 of R V, y 6 or 7 R VI, y 17 of R IX

Amennakht, and Harshire with brothers - year year 13 R IX, year 3 R X.

Khaemhedjet ii son of Harshire - y 3 R VI, y 10 & 17 RIX, y 3 R X, y 1 *whm mswt = y 19 R XI*

Thutmose (Dhutmose) son of Khaemhedjet ii, y 17 & 19 R IX, y 2 R X, y 8-28 R XI, but in y 10-12 *whm mswt* (= y 28-30 R XI), with scribe Iufnamun (unrelated).

Butehamun son of Thutmose with Thutmose y 20 R XI, y 10-12 *whm mswt* (y 28-30 R XI)

Butehamun with scribe (N)esamenope (unrelated) y 19 R XI.

Butehamun y 11-13 of king ? Herihor with HPA Pinudjem son of Piankh.

Ankhefenamun son of Butehamun y 16 of a king ? Herihor, with HPA Masaharta.

Nebhebit (brother of Ankhefenamun) y 20-21 king ? Herihor.

Scribes of Necropolis descendants of Amennakht X

HPA Pinudjem Masaharta

Herihor

whm mswt

whm mswt R XI Dyn 21 Dyn 21

R X R X R X R X

R IX R IX R IX R IX R IX

R VI R VI

R V

R VI R IV

R III R III

After Bierbrier 1975, and George Wood 2020

Even more revealing is the careers of scribe Kenherkhepeshef and his wife, followed by their descendants. p. 26.

1st working period			R II, and Siptah, and R V.
2nd	"	"	R III, and R V.
3rd	"	"	R IX.
4th	"	"	R XI.

Such indicates a closeness of R II, Siptah and R V. which brings problems for the conventional chronology.

HPA Ramessesnakht served year 1 of Ramses IV and also year 2 Ramses IX, his son- law Amenemopet 3 PA, P mut. was in office during reign of Ramses III to Ramses V.

Now on the linear graph this would place the son-in-law before the father-in-law, but on the revised chronology here, Amenemopet (son-in-law) would begin his office either at the same time as Ramessesnakht or slightly later, depending on which year of R III he began. Such makes more sense than a linear arrangement of all kings. It would also suggest a close start for both R III and R IV.

Kitchen also admits that R IV played "important roles at court before Year 27 of Ramses III." (p. 117). It would likely be year 27 on this revision that Ramses XI (Haq An), ascended the throne, if he followed R VII (Haq An), (+ the one year of R VIII).

The scene shown on theTheban Tomb of Amnemope -rear wall-A (Kitchen p. 116-7) - Ramses IV appears here in the presence of R III - year 27 minus (x+y) - which could easily be years 1-6 of R III corresponding to Rameses IV if appointed at beginning of R III's reign. The scene then does not contradict this revised scheme. Only the 3rd and 4th scenes refer to year 27.

A diagrammatic relationship would be as follows:-

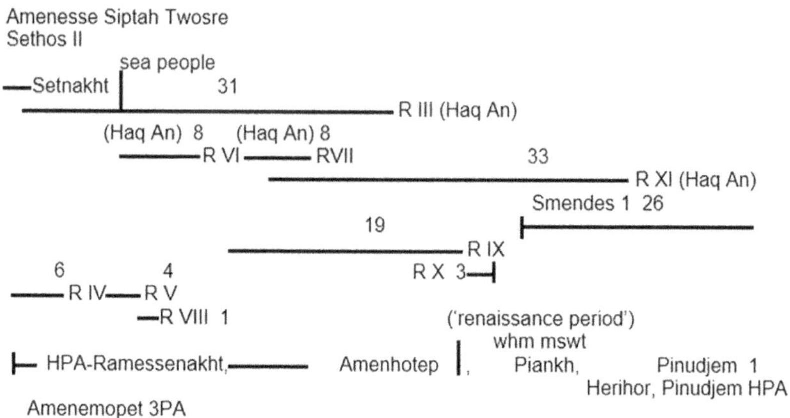

Of interest is the fact that a Prince Meryatum, was acting as High Priest of Re in Heliopolis during year 4 of Ramses V (Kitchen p. 123 JEA 68), Kitchen sees this as a different person from the Prince Meryatum appointed by R II in his 26th year, If Kitchen is correct, then Meryatum son of Ramses III -a nephew once removed of Meryatum son of Ramses II - would have almost certainly assumed the Priesthood in Heliopolis on the termination of Meryatum son of Ramses II . (Meryatum y 4 R V would be close to the time of the incursion of the Sea People in R III's 8th year - see later)

From Pap. Salt 124, and the details given by Bierbrier (p. 23 and 30) It is clear that Sethos II overlapped Ramses III, and the possibility is that year 6 of R III at least was concurrent or before year 5 of Sethos II, which also suggests that the Theban rule of Sethos began at about the same period as Ramses III, and well before Merenptah began his sole reign. In fact, Merenptah may well have placed him there at a time of rising conflict within the family of R II (while he attended to Memphis and Pi-Ramses). In other discussion I have placed this circa. 763 BC. i.e. 29 years into the reign of R II.

```
|? 763 BC
|     6    12 14    R III -31
***********|**|****************
 Sethos II  6                    Total period Sethos II to end Tausert = 14 years
     5
 ****|*                          Expiry then of that short lived Dynasty = y 15 R III
    **                                                             ? circa. 748 BC
  Amenesse

     ******
      Siptah  6
          **      | circa. 749 BC - approx. the last year of Sheshonk I
          Tausert  2
```

Ramses III faced the Sea People in year 8, which I have dated 755 BC, the only Rameside records found in the Palestinian area dated before the Sea people had terminated Egyptian control in the southern levant (if we are to accept Finkelstein's theory of two phases of control,- 1995), are of R III, IV, V and VI, which would allow R IV and VI were reigning close together in time during the early years of R III, but either in different areas or co-regent, (VI is Haq An, hence at Heliopolis, so likely co-regent, R IV ? somewhere in the eastern Delta + or - Thebes, attestations come from Wadi Hammamat, Serabit el-Khadim, and Heliopolis, as well as the southern Levant).

The presence of artefacts of R IV, R V and VI in Palestine would surround the conflict of R III in year 8. It is unlikely, given the tensions which would occur over that period that R IV and R V would be there other than with R III, and that would include R VI.

Given that the initial battle occurred in year 8 of R III, it is eminently possible that R IV was placed on the throne very early in the reign of R III followed soon after by R V his son., then R VI would come to the throne at Heliopolis around year 9, soon after the battle, and in charge of Heliopolis.

R VI reigned for 8 years, starting during R V's 3rd year, and was followed by his son R VII (also Haq An - Heliopolis) for 8 years.

The death of R VII on that scenario would be year 25 of Ramses III, and it is then likely that R XI who also bore the title Haq An, would then ascend the throne at Heliopolis in co-regent capacity with R III.

Ramses III was murdered in his 31st year, leaving R XI in charge at Heliopolis, thus starting his sole reign in his 6th year, then reigning for 30 more years (Thijs believes that was 33 years).

The total for the Dynasty then was 26 + 25 = 51 years (on standard acceptance) 54 years, if Thijs claims are correct.

The above suggestions make for at least 5 years overlap of R XI with R III.

End of Dynasty then 763 minus 51 = 712 BC. We have identified Piye at 711 BC, and there was no evidence of the 20th Dynasty at that time.

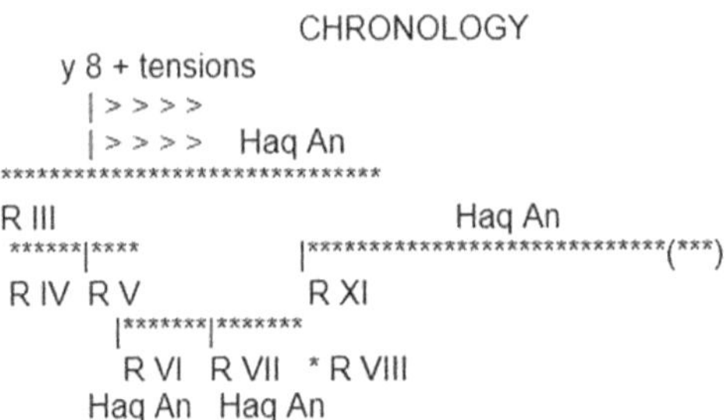

Four kings of 20th Dynasty had the title Haq An (Ruler of Heliopolis), if these are assumed to have followed sequentially then the time covered would be 31+8+8+33 = 80 years, but there clearly was overlap of R III, R VI and R VII, which would suggest that R VI and R VII were co-regent with R III, and followed by a partial co-regency of R XI.

We have more details available, for we know of the suppression of HPA Amenhotep year 17 R XI, and the beginning of the *whm mswt* (renaissance period) year 19 of R XI. The death of R X just before that and the death of R IX year 17 of Rameses XI.

20th DYNASTY PERIOD R III, R IX, R XI.

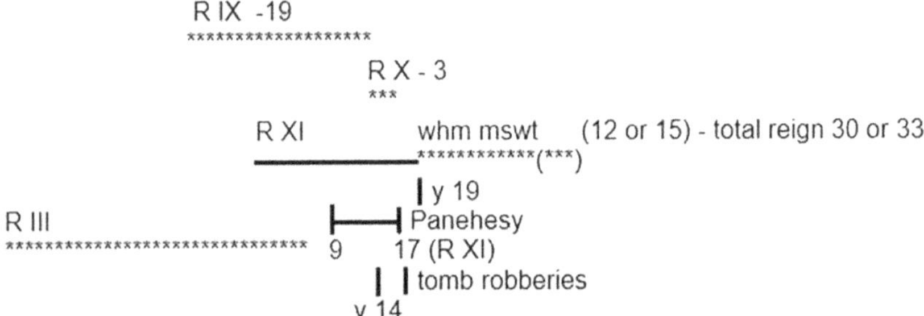

So a 12 year overlap of R IX and R III, and a 5 year overlap of R XI and R III.

The invasion by Panehesy, vice-roy of Kush, occurred in year 9 of Ramses XI provoking restless times. He is recorded in years 9,12, and 17 of R XI, and apparently 'suppressed the HPA Amenhotep, resultant turbulence followed, described as war, Panehesy was banished back to Kush and apparently for the moment Amenhotep was restored.

If then we go with this scenario - the murder of R III (perhaps around y 5-6 of R XI), followed by a turbulent period resulting also a few years later with the suppression of HPA Amenhotep, R XI taking the reigns and proclaiming the *whm mswt*, in his year 19, (reigning for another 15 years, equivalent to the 15 years of the whm mswt- although many claim 12 years) then the total reign of the Ramesides after Setnakht was close to 51, alternate 54 years.

We need to keep in mind that R IV, VI, VIII and likely R X and R XI were of the same generation, if the genealogy listed above is correct.

Clearly towards the end of the reign of R III turbulence set in, first the Harem conspiracy, and trials, involving wife Tiye and son Penteweret, but clearly there was restlessness among the sons of R III, for Thijs points out that R IV who did not hold the title Haq An, in y 2 of his reign adopted the epithet "the true/ legitimate one" and his son R V in Turin 2044 mentions "enemies" (probably Egyptians), which would reflect very early turbulence.

(a possible cause of this may well have been the struggle between Sethos II, Amenesse. Siptah and Twosre in Thebes, rather than foreign enemies - the time would be right)

R X who reigned only three years died at the time of the war (probably under Panehesy), the time of the suppression of HPA Amenhotep. year 17 of R XI, and I believe these events followed close after the murder of R III.

Thijs has placed R X's death after that of R IX (19 year reign), Thijs may well be right and makes a strong case for R X beginning his reign on the death of R IX.

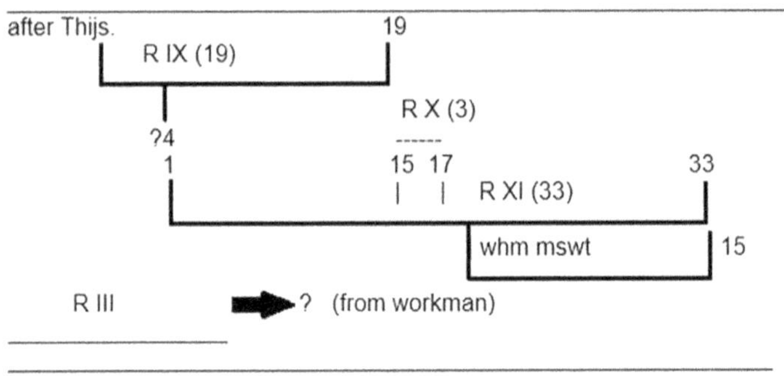

If one were to speculate a motive for these family convulsions it would likely be that the sons of chief wife Isis-Hamadjilit were the ones selected by R III to be early inheritors of the rule of their chief city Heliopolis (hence Haq An), the others confined to lesser regions / cities, and on each of their deaths of R VI and VII, R XI were sequentially made co-regent - Haq An.

The order of the turbulence then would be:-

Harem conspiracy, then murder of R III, Tomb Robberies, followed by the war under Panehsy, removal of the high priest Amenhotep, intervention by R XI, and if Thijs is correct Menkheperre with the assistance of Psusennes I, (Banishment stele), who had held northern jurisdictions, temporary assumption of HPA by Nesamun, proclamation of whm mswt (year 19 of R XI- year 1 of whm mswt) and R XI takes rule in Thebes, then return of Amenhotep, followed by Piankh (years 7-10 of whm mswt), then Herihor (Piankh's son as HPA, followed by Herihor's brother Pinudjem HPA (a separate person from his uncle king Pinudjem I), finally brother-in-law HPA Masaharta, during the reign of Herihor (21 years).

On death of R XI, now covering Thebes, Khakheperre Pinudjem would rule at Thebes (Karnak)- 10 years, followed by Herihor as king, who had placed brother Pinudjem as HPA

After Thijs:-

year 25 Psusennes 1 = year 17/18 of R XI = — start of whm mswt the next year.

year 40 Psusennes 1 = year 32/33 R XI = year 14 or 15 whm mswt.

then:-

Death of R X - year 17 R XI, death of R IX perhaps 3 years before, and death of R III circa. several years before that.

Now artefacts found in Levant belong to R III, R IV, R V and R VI only, and Finkelstein makes a case for the final movement from the Levant by the 20th Dynasty occurred after this and would be close to year 22(+) of R III (p. 216).

The only one not easily placed is the 1 year reign of Ramses VIII, conventionally placed after Ramses VII, and while this is logical, it is speculation only.

Now a possible objection to this shortened chronology of the 20th Dynasty would be the claim that there was not enough generational time for these kings. However, the evidence is strong that some if not many of the Pharaohs began their procreation in their teens.

Such is inferred by Kitchen's claims (1982 p.43) that Ramses II came to the throne aged 25 years, and p 39 states:-

> "*When crowned, he had been presented with a full-scale royal family. During the years of regency, the young 'king'* early began to rear quite a family."

It is clear that procreation had started early in Ramses II's teens.

Moreover, Ramses IV came to the throne aged 21, reigning 6 years, and was immediately followed by son Ramses V aged 13 years, which means that Ramses V had been born close to Ramses IV's 14th year of life.

If then Setnakht as a son of R II had been born in the teen years of R II and had himself procreated (R III) by his year 15, and so on each generation, the shortened chronology becomes very likely. Ramses III could have begun to rear a family around the 15th year of Ramses II or even slightly earlier, beginning his reign before the 30th year of Ramses II, soon placing the young Ramses IV on the throne in parallel elsewhere,? at Thebes, while he ruled at Heliopolis.

DYNASTY 20 and DYNASTY 19 CONUNDRUM

R III also finds himself contemporary with Amenesse (Amen.) and Siptah, and Sethos II (S II)- end Dynasty 19, and R XI, with Smendes I - Dynasty 21, who then extends beyond him.

Then we find R II and Sethos II associated with an early appearance of Merenptah- (Bierbrier. p 2), the family of Roma 1. That is:- S II and R II with Bakenkhons I, and Merenptah with his brother Ipuy I (suggested by Bierbrier to be a much younger son), which raises significant questions as to whether S II reigned before the death of of R II and whether Merenptah in fact had a co-regent period with his father before his sole reign. Such would fit with the timing of his contemporary Tuhaliyas IV of Hatti, who had a significant co-regency with father Hattusillis III during the later years of R II.

Merenptah was proclaimed crown prince year 55 of R II and took on more responsibilities as Prince Regent. This most likely gives credibility to the previous statement. In fact, Kitchen p. 112 states:-

> *"After the death of Prince Kwaemwaset, about year 55—. Already, Merenptah had in later years* been the king's right-hand-man in helping to manage affairs in Pi- Ramesse and the East Delta. Following Kwaemwaset's death, he extended his responsibilities as far as Memphis—"

It seems to me that there is no way of reconciling the above details without admitting serious parallelisms, and such would also suggest significant co-regencies. And Ramses IX -reign 19 years suggests his reign fell across the reigns of R III and Ramses XI.

Smendes also finds contemporaneity with Herihor and Pinudjem I, who all most likely overlap with R XI, (both Smendes and Pinudjem I married daughters of R XI)

The main Ramesides artefacts of the 20th Dynasty were found in the Egyptian territories in southern Palestine are from R III, R IV, R V and R VI, before the days of the Bichrome 'Philistine'(nee Sea people) ware, and also the earlier Monochrome ware, which appears to post-date those artefacts. (Finkelstein Israel, Tel Aviv 22, 1995).

REFERENCES

Bierbrier M.L. 1975. The late New Kingdom in Egypt. Aris & Phillips Ltd

Finkelstein, Israel. Tel Aviv 22 / 2, 1995. p. 213-239.

Kitchen K. 1982, Pharaoh Triumphant. Aris & Phillips Ltd Warminster England.

Kitchen, K. 1982 Journal Egyptian Archaeology, vol. 68, p.116 -125.

Manley, Bill, The Penguin Historical Atlas of Ancient Egypt, 1996, p. 134.

Papyrus Salt 124 (British Museum Papyrus 10055)

Wood, George, 2020, "The life and Times of Butehamun: Tomb Raider for the Priest of Amun" M.A. Thesis for Uppsala University. UPPSALA UNIVERSITET Institute of Archaeology and Ancient History.

PART 5

THE ASSUMED END OF THE 19TH DYNASTY, AND CONCURRENT DYNASTIES

ABSTRACT

A case will here be made that the end period of the 19th Dynasty embracing the reigns of Sethos II, Amenmesse, Siptah, and Twosre, did not in fact follow the reign of Merenptah, but was a short period parallel with the early period of the 20th Dynasty of Heliopolis, consisting of rule at Thebes involving family conflict between sons and grandsons of Ramses II, before the death of Ramses II, and before the sole reign of Merenptah.

KEYWORDS

Sethos II, Amenmesse, Siptah, Twosre, Ramses III.

The details of the assumed terminal 19th Dynasty are reasonably well established, in the conventional chronology.

Sethos II son of Merenptah took (or was appointed to) the throne in THEBES, where he reigned for about 6 years. Remember Merenptah was involved mainly with R II at Memphis and Pi-Ramses.

Sethos reign was interrupted in years 3 and 4 by the advent of Amenmesse (who I believe was another son of R II -Amenemua no. 8 of Petrie, and an uncle of Sethos II), who had taken control of Upper Egypt and Nubia. Such suggests a family conflict between Amenmesse and Merenptah - no. 13 of Petrie.

On the death of Sethos II, Siptah, son of Amenmesse, was appointed, at THEBES, apparently with the help of Chancellor Bay, who later was executed in Siptah's 5th year. Siptah apparently reigned 6 years.

Twosre then took the throne for about 2 years until her death, but her tomb had been usurped for the burial of Setnakht. These latter events occurred just around the 8th year conflict of R III with the Sea People, which I date circa. 755 BC.

The 20th Dynasty against this revised chronology then would become extinct circa. 718 -714 BC. i. e. covering circa. 763 - 714 BC, and so ending around the 25th year of Sheshonk III, whence Sheshonk III would take control of Heliopolis, and the title 'Haq An'.

A PROBLEM PRESENTS ITSELF

However the above details of the workman during the 20th Dynasty, gives us reason to suggest that this scenario was NOT in fact at the terminus of the 19th Dynasty, but occurred earlier during the reign of R II and before Merenptah's SOLE reign, as a brake-off from the 19th to take control of strategic areas while other areas were coming under other control by other sons of R II (e.g at Heliopolis). Merenptah himself was now well committed to Pi-Ramesse and then given responsibilities also at Memphis.

We need then to examine the life of Ramses II.

Kitchen.K.A. (Pharaoh Triumphant).

Kitchen p.43, suggests that Ramses II was about 25 years of age at sole enthronement.

p.39

> *"When crowned he had been presented with a full-scale royal household. During the years of the regency, the young 'king' early began to rear quite a family."*
>
> *"In ten years up to the death of Sethos I, they each presented Ramesses with at least five sons and a couple of daughters, while the lesser ladies of the harim (discreetly veiled from us) may have accounted for five or ten sons and as many more daughters."*

This suggested that the oldest son at Rameses accession was at least 10 years of age, (and up to 25 sons were living).

The important players in the reigns of the next few years were Kwaemwaset, he would die before assuming office, but his name suggests an association with Thebes.

Merenptah no. 13, who would be appointed Prince Regent year 55, but active also earlier and assumed SOLE office on the death of Ramses (here 727 BC). Clearly of significant age-at least 70.

Sethos II son of Merenptah, I am suggesting was placed in Thebes,? by Ramses II or by his father Merenptah, somewhere around 760 BC and could be aged in his early twenties or even older.

Amenmesse (son Amenemua no. 8 of R II - of Petrie), who would conflict with Sethos II (? nephew), and then have his son Siptah reign for 6 years, after the 6 year reign of Sethos II. Siptah would die about 16 years of age, and Twosre (most likely also a daughter of R II), would assume the throne for 2 years, and usurp the sarcophagus of Amenherkhepshef son of Ramses VI, who died age 15 before his father R VI.

Setnacht (most likely son of R II, Setnakhtamun, or Snechtenamun no. 20 of Petrie) to Heliopolis, who would then appoint son Ramses III (a little before 760 BC), to the throne in Heliopolis. Possible age of the latter unknown, but here could well be 25 years at accession.

The point being made here is that Dynasty 20, and the end reigns of Dynasty 19, usually attributed AFTER the death of Merenptah, occurred PRIOR to Merenptah coming to the throne for his sole reign.

As well, an earlier case was made for the appointment of the military leader we later recognise assuming royal title as Sheshonk I to Heracleopolis, Bubastis and perhaps Tanis around 770 BC, while Ramses II administered the country from Pi-Ramesse, and Memphis.

So, the beginning of Dyn 20, 22, and the assumed LATE Dyn. 19. began, close to the same time, and while Ramses II was still on the throne. The following discussion attempts to show the details, but the discussion also embraces the appearance of the "Sea People".

FURTHER CLARIFICATIONS

1) As discussed above Setnakht, founder of the 20th dynasty, can most likely be set against Azariah's (Uzziah) reign, and I have suggested before 755 BC.

The early part of this dynasty is close to the time of the appearance of the "Sea People" and also sits in archaeological horizon just after the end of the Late Bronze period, and beginning of Iron 1 period in the Levant.

(As an aside, it is obvious by this revision that this author rejects the false concept of a Bronze Age collapse, assumed because of the elasticised sequential chronology of the 3rd Intermediate Period', here I agree with David Rohl, Peter James and Nel Weggalaar, that this is a modern artificial construct)

In Palestine a significant archaeological horizon which brings these features together is destruction level XIV at Ashdod, which I attribute to Uzziah (Azariah) as mentioned in 2 Chron. 26:6-7, not to the Sea People, and therefore most likely close to the time of the beginning of the 20th Dynasty. While the Bible refers to Ashdod as a Philistine city- which it was, it was also an Egyptian fortress during that period, and on this revision would fit with an attack by Uzziah prior to his possible conflict with Setnakht, or alternately as a action taken with awareness of the approaching Sea People.

In discussion of Ashdod level XIV, and similar time local destructions, Finkelstein (1995) makes the comment- p.229 I" *It is far from clear whether these sites were destroyed contemporaneously.*"

It is the layer above this where we first find the appearance of the Sea People (incorrectly labelled Philistines), who would amalgamate their culture with the Philistines. Itamar Singer Tel Aviv 12-2. 1985. p. 110:- "*The Monochrome pottery appears at Ashdod in the first phase of Stratum XIII (XIIIb) and is gradually replaced by Bichrome Philistine pottery in the second phase of this stratum (XIIIa) (M.Dothan 1972:5, 1981b:152-153, T Dothan 1982a:96, 294)*

It is close to this level therefore that Rameses III's conflict with the Sea people occurred, and again I would locate this event close to 755 BC. I then relate level XI to Sargon II's attack on Ashdod.

I would suggest that Ashdod was first controlled by Uzziah prior to settlement of Sea People, and his attack and setting up of towns in the area may well have been partly in anticipation of the oncoming threat of the Sea People.Then their settlement began to occur after his disability and during Jotham's reign, and particularly during Ahaz reign.

The tale of Wenamun, which has often been dismissed as a fictional production, I believe has too much historical detail to be branded as such, and I would place it during the era of Tiglath-Pileser III (TG III, 745-727 BC).

In that tale we have the High Priest of Amun (believed to be Herihor, who is mentioned in the tale), Smendes I and wife Tentamun B daughter of Ramses XI, we have the fact that the Sea people had already arrived on coastal Palestine and were settled in Dor and clearly had ships on the sea. We meet a prince of Byblos who is called in Wenamun's pronunciation Zakarbaal, and who may well be the Shipitbaal (but pronounced phonetically by Wenamun, or less likely a possible successor) during the days of Tiglath -Pileser III.We hear that there is coastal trade with one 'Wereker' (Waraktir) who is very likely Urikki of Kue, also contemporary with TG III and Shipitbaal. There is also mention of one Khaemwaset, whose servants after 17 years of mistreatment at Byblos were previously slain, and this person is very likely the earlier crown prince of Ramses II.

Why then did the Byblos prince deal so roughly with Wenamun ?- most likely because he was now under the hegemony of the Assyrian Tiglath-Pileser III, whom he had no intention of upsetting - knowing the almost certain consequences.

Which king then does the year 5 belong to? Ramses XI and Smendes are both possible, but Smendes is a recipient in Tanis, and the letter is from the High Priest of Amun in Thebes. This leaves 2 other likely candidates Herihor and Pinudjem I who were contemporary. Of those two, it appears that Herihor is most likely at that moment, although the tale is assumed to be set in the time of his High Priesthood, when Khepekhare Pinudjem I was ruling in Thebes and Ramses XI had just recently died, but Smendes was still alive in Tanis That scenario embraces all the Egyptian notaries of the tale.

This period is also just after the contemporary reign with Sheshonk I. So, we would place it just after the reign of Sheshonk I, and during the early years of Orsorkon II, perhaps close to 730 BC.

2) A significant problem appears around the end of 19th Dynasty- let me explain.

The conventional order is Ramses II, Merenptah, Sethos II apparently parallel with Amenmesse, then Siptah and finally Twosre.

It would of course be expected that Sethos II Amenmesse, Siptah would be in the same close time frame as the early days of Setnakht / Ramses III.

In any discussion of workmen and priests related to these reigns we would then expect clear mention of Merenptah - a significant king. But such appears not to be the case.

Referring to Biebrier "The Late New Kingdom in Egypt" 1975, the following is found:-

1) The family of the foreman Neferhotep, P 21.
   Two time periods of Ramses II then one time period with Sethos II and Ramses II, then Ramses II and Siptah. but no mention of Merenptah.

N.B. Bierbrier suggests that Merenptah was involved p.21, but his reference note 18, makes it clear that the document involved does NOT mention a Pharaoh's name, and Bierbrier's conclusion therefore is made then from the conventional chronology.

2) The family of workman Pashedu p.24
Two consecutive time periods of Ramses II then two periods of Amenmesse and Siptah, but no mention of Merenptah.
The family of Sennedjem p.30.

3) consecutive time periods of Ramses II, followed by Amenmesse and Ramses III, then Sethos II, Ramses III and Ramses IV. No mention of Merenptah.

4) The family of Kaha p. 36
Two consecutive workmen periods a) Ramses II then again Ramses II, the next is Amenmesse, Siptah, and Ramses III but no mention of Merenptah.

In fact in the family of Neferhotep, R II is placed in the same time frame as Sethos II and Siptah. Such goes contrary to conventional thinking, for Ramses II should be dead years before.

Added to this is the family of High Priest of Nekhbet, Setau, then son-in-law, HPA Ramessesnakht, and then daughter Aatmerit married to grandson of Bakenkhonsu Amenemopet, thus 3 generations contemporary with 20th Dynasty kings, but also contemporary with Bakenkhonsu who was in service to Ramses II, and all of this before Merenoptah, this demands most of Dynasty 20 was before the reign of Merenptah. Such conflicts with accepted dogma.

Now there can be no doubt that Merenptah followed Ramses II, but it should at this stage be stated that he acted as Prince regent for some years before, during the later reign of Ramses II. According to Kitchen he was also active before becoming Prince regent at the death of Khaemweset in y 55, exactly what capacity is not fully known but one cannot rule out foreign relations, such as that with Tudhaliyas IV, of Hatti. In fact Kitchen p. 112, claims that Merenptah "*For the final twelve years of his aged father's reign, Merenptah was the real ruler of the kingdom, virtually pharaoh in all but name."*

But Amenmesse, Siptah and Sethos II in these genealogies are related in time to Ramses II and Ramses III.This seems to indicate that these kings did not in fact follow Merenptah but were associated with Ramses II earlier, and also at the time of the separate set-up of the 20th Dynasty during Ramses II's reign. Was the 20th Dynasty in fact set up at Heliopolis by Ramses II, (or independently) by his suggested son Snechtenamun (Setnakht, Setnakhtamun)?. At a similar time Merenptah's son Sethos II in conflict with possible uncle Amenmesse (son of R II Amenemua of Petrie), set up at Thebes, (and so involving a family conflict), and earlier than the end of Ramses II's reign?. Here a comfortable time would be soon close to Ramses II's 34th year (the marriage to the Hittite princess - on this revision 758 BC). Some of the earlier sons would already have sons, even into late teens or early twenties.

Ramses II had appointed son Meryatum as priest in Heliopolis, around or after year 26 (776 BC) on this revision, it is not unreasonable to suggest that Snechtenamun (here Setnakht), was soon appointed or took control to rule Heliopolis, at least around year 34 (758 BC) or before, and envious actions by brothers Merenptah (through son Sethos II) and Amenemua (here suggested a possible candidate for Amenmesse) took control of Thebes, producing the known conflict, (Merenptah was heavily involved elsewhere under Ramses II with Memphis and Pi-Ramses).

I am then suggesting that the aged Merenptah's reign at Memphis and Pi-Ramses was therefore later than Amenmesse / Siptah / Sethos II's family conflict in Thebes many years before, concurrent with the beginning of the 20th Dynasty which was then being ruled by Ramses XI by the time of Merenptah.

The conflict of Ramses III with the Sea people -year 8- appears to be earlier? 755 -760 BC and related to the LB II / Iron 1 interface. Whereas Merenptah's conflict in year 5 (definitely Iron 1) was 722 BC at the time of the end of Northern Israel, but was in the west against rising Libyan (and Sea People) groups, who, though temporally stopped soon rose under Tefnakht 1 against Piye 711 BC and the start of Dynasty 24. Merenptah by this revision dying in 717 -18 BC.

I feel Azariah of Judah still holds the most reasonable candidacy for 'Arsu the Syrian', rather than Chancellor Bay, as often suggested.

This revision also makes sense of the order of the kings holding title- Haq An - in order Ramses III then VI, then VII, then XI followed by Sheshonk III, Sheshonk IV, and Sheshonk V. This also allows the possibility that Ramses XI died during the early years of Sheshonk III, we need to remember that one of the titles of Ramses XI was 'Haq An'- his rule was from Heliopolis, before his rise in Thebes.

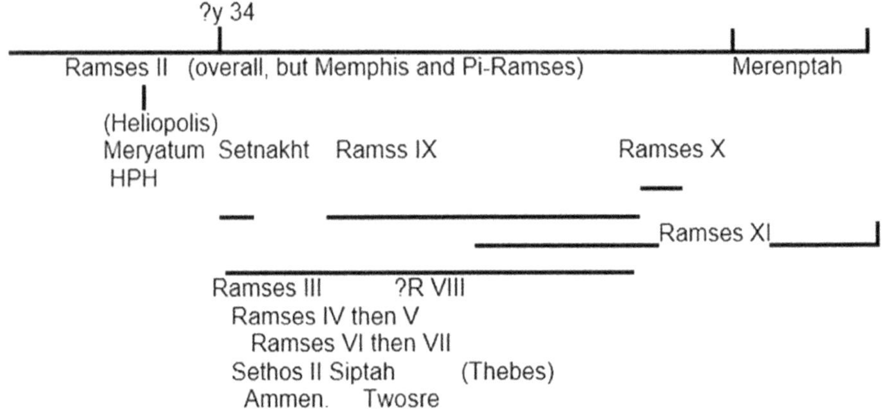

CONCLUSION

The 'end', then of Dynasty 19 occurred in the city of Thebes and ran its course as the 20th Dynasty was in its early throes in Heliopolis, events that transpired before Merenptah began his sole reign, in Memphis and Pi-Ramses.

I quote Gardiner, 1963, p.46:-

> "*If the foregoing interpretations of the all too scanty data are correct, then the history of the later Nineteenth Dynasty will be seen to be nearer to that reconstruction proposed many years ago by de Rouge', who postulated that Amenmesse and Siptah formed a sort of sub-dynasty of their own intercalated within the larger period. The feud in*

the royal house doubtless arose as a result of the long reign of Ramses II who outlived the older of his many sons,—"

To that I would agree, except to add that Amenesse and Siptah were a sub-dynasty within another sub-dynasty created by feuds within the royal house, but well before the death of Ramses II and the sole reign of Merenptah, and the major players were Amenmesse and Merenptah.

In the overall scheme then, it is possible that the end of this sub-dynasty just preceded the reign of Harsiese A of Dynasty 22 (pre-Dyn. 23).

THE CHARACTERS

1) SETHOS II, son of Merenptah, would probably be in his twenties at enthronement.

consort Twosre, sons Seti Merenptah and unnamed daughter, both died young. names :-

Horus - *ka nakht wer pehty* - The strong bull great of might.

Nebty - *Nakht khepesh der pedjut 9* - The strong one who has repelled the 9 bows

- *mek kemetwaf khasut* - The protector of Egypt who has subdued foreign countries.

Golden Horus - *Aa neru em tau nebu* - he whose victories are great in all lands

Throne - *User kheperu Ra (Setep en Ra), variant - mery Amun, mery Seth*

Powerful are the manifestations of Ra, chosen of Ra, beloved of Amun, beloved of Seth.

Birth - *Seti Merenptah* - The one who belongs to Seth, beloved of Ptah.

Reigned for 6 years interrupted years 3 and 4 by Amenmesse.

2) AMENMESSE (meaning - born or fashioned by Amun) - here believed to be a son of Ramses II no. 8. of Petrie. Names indicate he had high claims on Thebes names:-

Horus - *Ka nakht merymaat semen tawy* - Strong bull beloved of maat who strengthens the two lands.
Nebty - *Wer biaut mi Ipet-sut* - He who is great of miracles in Karnak Temple.
Golden Horus - Aa khepesh saa Waset en mes su - The one great of might who has magnified Thebes for the one who bore him.
Throne - *Men mi Ra setep en Ra* - Eternal like Ra, the chosen one of Ra
Birth - *Amenmesse (mery Ra) heqa Waset* - The beloved of Ra, ruler of Thebes.

2a) Another candidate for Amenmesse is the grandson of prophet and later HPA Bakenkhonsu, brother of Paser and Nefertari, Amenesse (sometimes called Amenmose and attested y 3 Ramses IV- Bierbrier p.11) who became governor of Thebes, as well as being prophet of Amun and chief taxing master (Bierbrier p.11). On this revised chronology the time agrees. Amenesse of Dyn. 19 held the title "Ruler of Thebes", and as brother of vizier and prophet Paser and Nefertari wife of 3PA Tjanefer, the possibility of a usurpation from this man occurring must be considered (such an event is not a new suggestion here). Paser was mayor of Thebes in year 16 of Ramses IX (but is also attested earlier y's 2, 3 and 18 Ramses III, and as such on this revision Amenmesse would correlate to the revised time of end Dyn.19 and days of Ramses III. Amenemopet 3PA husband of Nefertari was also active at the period of Ramses III and V.

He and his brother and sister could well be born as children of the daughter of Bekenkhonsu, who at that time could be in her low twenties allowing these children to be also at least in their twenties around or after the 30th year of R II. Often when thinking about generations we forget that several generations can be contemporary even though the ages are different.

We do not know who Bakenkhonsu's daughter was married to, but Bakenkhonsu did bear the title "god's father" and the mother of Amenesse of Dyn.19 was said to have been Takhat - "King's daughter", "king's mother" and apparently over the first "King's wife", the whole area still remains with many questions.

Adding to the mystery is the claims that Chancellor Bay who helped Siptah to the throne is considered by some to be a relative of a Caananite princes Sutailya (or Soteraya) apparently Hurrian, who may have been married to either Seti II or Amenmesse, again the matter is unresolved. The cessation of the building of Bay's tomb was stated by "scribe of the tomb Paser". Amenesse himself had an HPA Roma called Roy (under R II Merenptah and Sethos II).

3) SIPTAH (meaning - son of Ptah), assumed son of Amenmesse, reigned 6 years, and died about age 16 years, helped to the throne by Chancellor Bay, who was later executed in year 5. Twosre was Consort names:
   - Horus - *Ka nakht mery Hapy (sankh ta neb em kaef Ra neb)* - Strong bull beloved of Hapi who daily sustains the lands by means of his Ka.
   - (Variant) *Ka nakht wer pehty* - strong bull great of might.
   Nebty - *Saa Iunu* - made great in Heliopolis.
   Golden Horus - *mi itef Ra* - like his father Ra
   Throne - *Sekha en Ra meryamun* - he whom Ra causes to appear, beloved of amun - (variant) - *Akh en Ra setep en Ra* - Akh spirit of ra chosen of Ra.
   Birth - *Ramessu Si Ptah* - Ramessu son of Ptah
   changed to Si Ptah Mery en Ptah - MerenPtah son of Ptah

One can only ponder the change of Birth Name - perhaps it became politic after his enthronement and marriage to Twosre.

4) TWOSRE (Tausert, Tausret) origin unknown but likely a late daughter of Ramses II, originally married to Sethos II, then to Siptah, but evidence suggested that this latter arrangement was not without coercion. reigned 2 years after death of Siptah. Her tomb was usurped by Setnakht.
   Titles:- King's great wife
   Lady of the two lands
   Mistress of Upper and Lower Egypt
   Hereditary Princess. (Gardiner, 1954, p.42)
   Horus - *Ka nakht meryt maat (nebet en em nesu Atum)* - strong bull beloved of maat, (lord beautiful of kingship like Atum)

Nebty - *Gereg kemet waf khasut* - founder of Egypt who vanquishes foreign countries.

Throne - *Sitre merytamun - mery en Mut, setep en Mut* - daughter of Ra, beloved of Atum, beloved of Mut chosen by Mut.

Birth - *Tausret.*

This queen is almost certainly a daughter of Ramses II, Petrie sites a daughter whom he called Tausr?l p. 38.

THE SEA PEOPLE STORY - an upside - down chronology, during this period.

This hinges on another historical conundrum - that of the sea people, related in time here.

The first attack of these people was during the 8th year of Ramses III -approx. 755 BC, this despite the usual chronology was over 30 years before the attack during the 5th year of Merenptah - 722 BC, and about 11 years later was the attack by the Libyan chief Tefnakht I at the time of Piye.- 711 BC, at which time a Libyan Dynasty Dyn. 22 had been in power for some time in Egypt.

REFERENCES

Bierbrier, M.L. The Late New Kingdom in Egypt, 1975, Aris & Philips Ltd, Warminster, England

Gardiner Sir Alan, 1954 JEA Journal of Egyptian Archaeology vol. 40 p 40-44, The Tomb of Queen Twosre.

1963 JEA Journal of Egyptian Archaeology vol. 49, p. 41-48, The Parentage of King Siptah.

Kitchen K.A. Pharaoh Triumphant, 1982, Aris & Philips Ltd Warminster, England.

Petrie, Sir Flinders, History of Egypt Vol. III, 1905, Methuen & Co. London.

PART 6

24th DYNASTY

ABSTRACT

The 24th Dynasty is another of the Egyptian Dynasties that has been caught up and scrambled by the standard chronology, it is here clarified but is mixed in the Manetho records among the kings of the 24th and early 26th Dynasties.

KEYWORDS

Sais, Tefnakht and descendants.

The first person to come to mind concerning the 24th Dynasty is the Libyan leader Tefnakht I who conflicted with Piye 711 BC.

Even with this leader there is some controversy, because many believe that there was a second Tefnakht (the Stephinates / Stephinathis of Manetho), and the official names of the two are often confused.

The view taken here, which will soon be discussed, is that there were in fact 2 Tefnakhts as follows;-

Tefnahht I- *Wahibre, Iribre.* contemporary with Piye, and son of Gemnefsutkapu.

Tefnakht II - *Shepsesre.* contemporary with Sheshonk V.

Manetho's records: -	Dyn 24	Bochchoris of Sais for 6 (44) years.	
Gardiner state p. 449 -	Dyn 24	Shepsesre Tefnakhte	sole date yr. 8
		Wahkare Bekenrinef	sole date yr. 6
p. 451	Dyn 26	Eusebius	
		1) Ammeris the Ethiopian	12 years
		2) Stephinathis	7 years
		3) Nechepsos	6 years
		4) Nechao	8 years

There can be no doubt of 4), he is Necho I last of the 24th Dynasty, conquered by Assurbanipal in 664 BC (ARAB 2-771) and set back on the throne, dying soon after.

There is little dispute regarding Tefnakht 1 (except which name to apply), for he is clearly referred to on the Pianki Stela (Piye), but because Piye is, in conventional thinking, related to Sheshonk V rather than Sheshonk III, and as Tefnakht II's name appeared on a stela mentioning Sheshonk V, they have been assumed to be the same person. Such has been objected to particularly by Oliver Perdu (2002), who noted the similarity of Stela in year 2 of Necho I, and year 8 of Shepsesre. Dan'el Kahn has discussed this but still assuming that Piye attacked during the reign of Sheshonk V and pointed out that that king's donation stela of year 38 has similarities.

When, however, the invasion of Piye is placed back in its rightful place to the reign of Sheshonk III, it becomes clear that Shepsesre is in fact Tefnakht II and the likely father of Necho I.

And we can then assert that he reigned at least 8 years (7 claimed by Manetho), but as we proceed, it appears that his reign was much longer than that.

The best way to set the timing, is to look at the invasion of Assurbanipal in 664 BC, at which stage we discover a Patubishti (Pedubast) king of Sa'nu (Tanis) (ARAB 2-772), who is almost certainly Pedubast II, son of Sheshonk V who reigned for 10 years and almost certainly that reign was terminated by Assurbanipal.

As we know that Necho I was also contemporary, reigning for 8 years, and dying soon after re-appointed by Assurbanipal, we can then date Pedubast II to 674-664 BC, and Necho I to 672-664 BC.

Then the period 711 BC - time of Piye' s invasion, until 672 BC, needs discussion.

How long Tefnakht I reigned before Bakenrenef / *Wahkare* (Bocchhoris) came to power is uncertain but held to end not long after Piye's invasion, but it may well be that Tefnakht placed Bakenrenef on the throne of Sais as he ruled the rest of the western delta while he was still alive. So Bakenrenef - 711-705 BC, when he is claimed to have been executed by Shebitko in that king's second year - 705 BC.

Shebitko apparently appointed a Nubian vassal called by Manetho - Ammeris (Eusebius version), about whom little is known. A claimed 12 years- hence 704 - 693 BC.

If that is correct, he was replaced by Tefnakht II, as mentioned before, the possible father of Necho I.

However, Manetho next refers to a Nechepsos / Nechao (believed to be Nekauba - and given a 6 year reign), - *Menibre nekauba.* Father unknown but reasoned to possibly be Tefnakht II, and thought to be brother, therefore of Necho I.

Following him is Necho 1.

So, we place Nekauba 676 - 671 BC.

Suggesting a reign of Tefnakht II - *Shepsesre*, from 692 until 677 BC- 16 years.

However, as Tefnakht II is mentioned in Sheshonk's 38th and last year - 674 BC, it maybe that Nekauba assumed the throne a couple of years before Tefnakht's death.

OVERALL CONCLUSION OF THIS REVISION PARTS 1 TO 6

This revision asserts the possibility of a debilitated Ramses II for up to 30 years of the latter part of his reign, with the regionalisation of his kingdom to which he still ruled in name over Memphis and Pi-Ramses with his son Merenptah, who then would take the sole throne 726 BC, dying 716 BC with the termination of Dynasty 19.

As has been indicated the 20th Dynasty at Heliopolis and the "assumed " end of the 19th Dynasty, starting with Sethos II at Thebes, were side or break-off Dynasties during the reign of Ramses II and during his incapacity.The Tanite 22nd Dynasty ruling initially at Heracleopolis, Bubastis, then Tanis on appointment by Ramses II of Sheshonk in some capacity, then claiming kingship.Becoming the dominant but not sole dynasty of the "Third Intermediate Period", a period of fragmentation, but still strong dynasties.

From 711 BC it would fall under the hegemony of the 25th Kushite Dynasty, following Piye's invasion particularly in conflict with founder of the 24th Dynasty Tefnakht I, through to the rule of Necho I, followed in 664 BC, with the Assyrian invasion of Assurbanipal of Assyria.

REFERENCES

Aston, David. A. 1989 Journal of Egyptian Archaeology, 75, p.139- 154, "Takeloth II - A King of the Theban Twenty- third Dynasty ?."

ARAB, Luckenbill, Daniel David, 1927, Ancient Records of Assyria and Babylonia Vol. II, Greenwood Press, New York

Gardiner, Sir Alan. 1961, Egypt of the Pharaohs, Oxford Paperbacks, Oxford at the Clarendon Press.

Kahn, Dan'el, (2007), "The Transition from Libyan to Nubian Rule in Egypt: revisiting the Reign of Tefnakht", In the Libyan period in Egypt, Historical and Cultural Studies into the 21st-24th Dynasties: Proceedings of a Conference at Leiden University 25-27 October 2007 pp. 139 - 148.

Perdu, Oliver, 2002, De Stephinates a Nechao ou les debuts de la XXVie dynastie.

Comptes redus des seances de l'Academie des Inscritions et Belles-Lettres 146(4) p 1215-1244.

PART 7

SUMMARY AND DATES OF RULERS - AN OVERALL CHRONOLOGY OF 3rd INTERMEDIATE PERIOD

ABSTRACT

Following parts 1-6, I will now attempt to draw together the details of the Third Intermediate Period. And set it against the background first of the latter reign of Ramses II and Merenptah, then against the background soon after of the Kushite 25th Dynasty until the conquest of Egypt by Assyrian Assurbanipal 664 BC. Suggesting that those two dynasties followed one another with only about a 5 year break between them, the kings of the 25th Dynasty attacking AFTER the collapse of the 19th.

An appropriate starting point is to identify significant people in the list of kings of Egypt found in Assurbanipal's conquest list- ARAB -2, 771.

KEYWORDS

Parallel Dynasties, Late 19th through to 25th Dynasty.

The third intermediate period has been a contentious issue, earlier, and by many still, seen to last around 500 years. Some recent archaeologists and Egyptologists have begun to break with the accepted system, most on specific time periods, while some have realised that a significant break with the standard chronology may be appropriate.

Kenneth Kitchen's monumental work "The Third Intermediate Period in Egypt" still remains a gold mine of information, but serious questions surround his overall chronology.

David Rohl has made a radical break and given reasons for 21st and 22nd Dynasty contemporaneity, however I question some of his basic overall parameters, in arriving at dates.

David Aston JEA 75 has shown significant parallelisms around the time of Orsorkon II.

Peter James in his publication "Centuries of Darkness" has also made the case for a revision.

Ad Thijs has given a refreshing new approach to the 21st and 20th Dynasty overlap, and others have made advances, but as yet no one has been able to give a comprehensive overall review.

This discussion has attempted this but obviously rests on the significant work of those who have gone before. So let us summarise and hopefully arrive at more workable dates and arrangements of these Dynasties and kings.

Kenneth Kitchen's monumental work -"The Third Intermediate Period" defined this period following the 20th Dynasty of the Ramesides - Thus 21st to 25th Dynasties inclusive. His work rests strongly on a serial interpretation of the conventional chronology of those periods.

The revised chronology presented here, however, makes a case for this period being a period of fragmentation of the previous Monolithic 18th to 19th Dynasties, beginning during the later reign of Ramses II. A period when for some unstated reason Ramses II became less visible and may well have suffered from some disability.

The revision here then begins approximately 770 BC here equated around the early 30's of Ramses II's reign somewhere around the time of his marriage to the daughter of Hittite Hattusillis III and ends in agreement with Kitchen at the conquest by Assyrian Assurbanipal 664 BC - a period then, by this revision, of just under 110 years.

The revision presents some surprising and no doubt challenging conclusions that Dynasty 20 and the end of Dynasty 19 (Sethos II to Tausert) did not in fact follow Ramses II and Merenptah but were parallel as subsidiary dynasties during the mid and late reign of Ramses II, at Heliopolis and Thebes respectably.

The foundation for the dates and conclusions arrived at here rests on the authors claim that Ramses II reign was 792 - 727 BC. That an overlap occurred in the later reign of Ramses II with administrations of the 3rd Intermediate Period, possibly as a result of some incapacity of Ramses II

Such allows only a maximum period for the 3rd Intermediate Period of approximately 110 years (from circa. 770 - 664 BC).

This then demands significant parallels in that period and allows the possibility that a number of the later kings of that period are mentioned by Assurbanipal, at his conquest 664 BC, but being dislocated from their context by conventional thinking.

This whole period covers the Iron 1 and II period in Palestine (beginning during the Jehu Dynasty), the earlier 18th Dynasty largely covering the Palestinian Late Bronze. This means then, that Rohl's claim of Ramses II being the Shishak of the Bible simply does not correlate, he is too late.

Chronology summary

FIRST - and foremost we start with the 25th Dynasty:-

Year 664 BC- Assurbanipal conquered an Egypt overruled by Taharqa who came to the throne 690 BC- that is the last assured date working backwards for our Egyptian conventional chronology.

Taharqa superseded Shabako of 14 years (dying in his 15th year) - however a Karnak inscription is known to have Shabako 2nd year carved over Shebitko's 3rd year, which may explain Apis buried in year 6 Bakenranef (who died in his year 6),corresponding to Shabako's 2nd year Apis instillation -Apis 25- (Kitchen - table

20 p. 489), the latter dying year 14 Shabako. This latter date, on this revision, corresponds to year 2 Pimay.

Shebitko is now known to have reigned during Sargon II of Assyria, years 707-705 BC.

Prior was Piye, and his highest assured date is year 24., which then brings his invasion in his 20th year to 711 BC - This date is seminal in this revision.

Fugitive Iamani of Ashdod was surrendered by Shebiko 707 BC.

Boccorus (Bakenrenef 24th Dynasty) slain by Shebitko 705 BC.

Shabako engages Sennacherib at Eltekeh 701 BC, and is defeated, Sennacherib then attacks Hezekiah, who on this first occasion capitulates, (2 Kings 18:13-16).

Sennacherib attacks Hezekiah the second time 689 BC (Shea 1985), Taharqa mobilises but the battle is not joined, Sennacherib's army destroyed as recorded in the Bible.

Esarhaddon attacks Egypt, then later Assurbanipal attacks Egypt, summarily deals with rebels, then sets up Necho I.

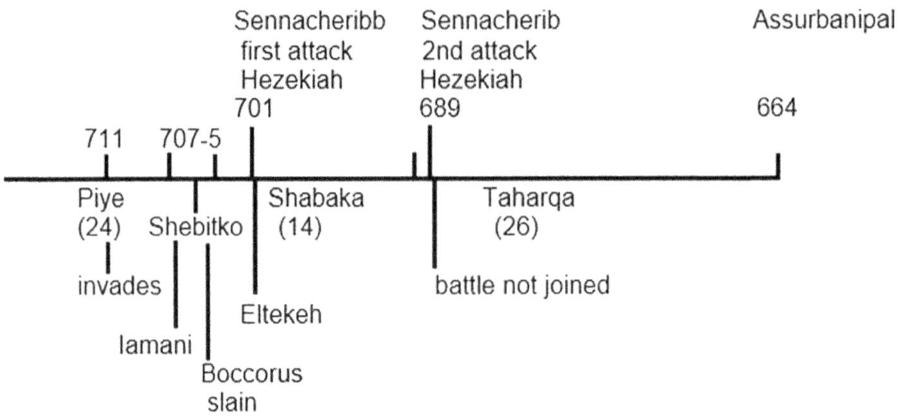

Apis Stela for burial Apis bull in year 14 of Taharqa (claimed born year 11, installed year 12 of Sheshonk V and living 26 years -calculated but NOT stated), however year 14 Taharqa will equate in time with the Apis Stela 31, 37th year of Sheshonk V. Correspondingly year 11 of Sheshonk V would equate here with close to year 2 Shabako, whose year 2 was written over Shebitko's year 3 (NLR 30

Karnak, and NLR 33 Karnak - the same year Bakenranef died). This suggests an extraordinary situation of overlap of Bakenranef -> Shabako Apis bulls at the same time of the later years of Apis installed year 28 of Sheshonk III. Such a situation may be explained by the Dynastic chaos precipitated by the Tefnakht / Piye conflict, and would be likely a unique event, precipitated by the 24th and soon 25th Dynasty takeover of Memphis, and that during the long reign of Sheshonk III, who was 'chief of the Ma at Busiris', but also ruling over Tanis.

It also indicates that Apis mentioned year 11, then year 37 Sheshonk V is in fact two Apis, a) installed year 2 Shabako (after death of the 5-6 year Bakenranef Apis) same as year 11 Sheshonk V, dying year 14 Shabako - aged 12 years, b) then Apis installed and dying year 14 Taharqa -14 years (the two adding up to 26 years - I repeat the 26 years assumed here are from calculation NOT any statement, and therefore it is not unreasonable to allow 2 Apis).

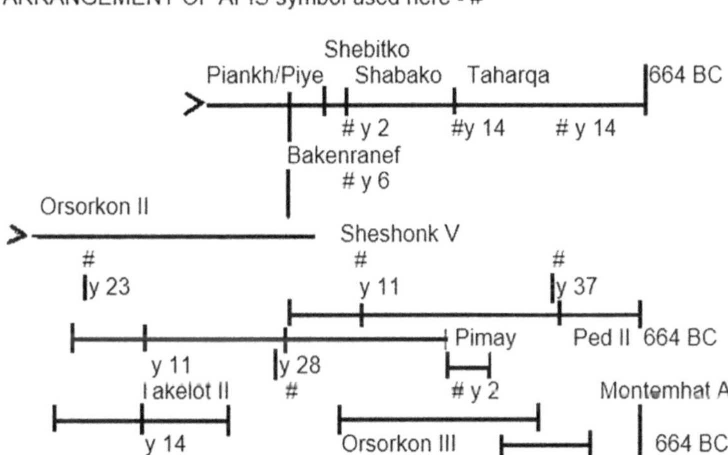

LEGEND Apis events indicated by # above.

Apis 18 died y 23 Orsorkon II

Apis 22 " y 14 Takelot II

Apis 22 died y 28 Sheshonk III age ? 17 years (from y 11- same as y 14 Takelot II)

Apis 22 installed y 28 Sheshonk III died y 2 Pimay - stated 26 years

Apis 24 died y 5, buried y 6 Bakenranef
Apis 25 installed y 2 Shabako = after Apis 24, died y 14 Shabako - 12 years.
Apis newly discovered died y 14 Taharqa -so 14 years following Apis 25
Apis 27 installed y 11 Sheshonk V,
Apis 31 died y 37 Sheshonk V Apis 27 + 31 = 2 Apis i.e Apis 25 + Apis y 14 Taharqa

---

SECOND - the 24th Dynasty:-

Bakenrenef (*Wahkare)* - Manetho's Bochchoris) was executed by Shebitko in that kings second year and Bakenrenef's 6th year -705 BC, giving the latter king's accession 711 BC, most likely placed there by Tefnakht I (*Wahibre, iribre)*), who had retreated to the western Delta.

In 664 BC Assurbanipal's records listed Necho I (ARAB 2, 771), and so working backward via Nekauba (Necheropses of Manetho), then Tefnakht II (Shepsesre), then Ammeris the Ethiopian to Bakenranef, we arrive close to the same date, circa 711 BC - Piye's invasion.

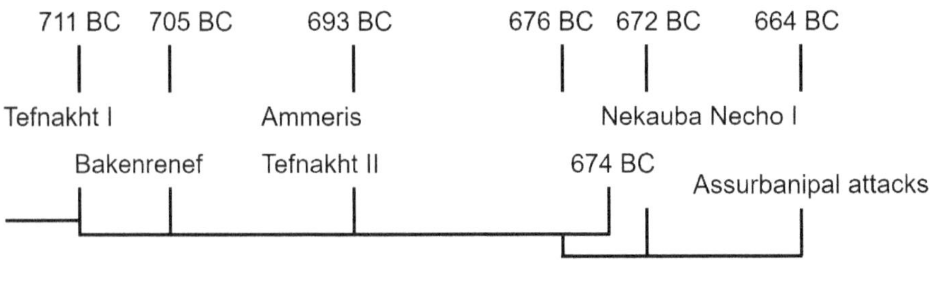

THIRD - the 21st Dynasty:-

Psusennes II, almost certainly the 'Bukkunanni'pi king of Hathiribi' (Arthribis) - ARAB 2, 771, mentioned by Assurbanipal (mistakenly called Bakeneffi D by Kitchen sect. 357), reigning 13 years, so back then to Siamun 17 years, Osorchor 6 years, then Amenope 9 years.- total 45 years brings us to 709 BC, a couple of years before the death of Psusennes I, whose name is not mentioned by Piye, but very contemporary with Orsorkon II who is the likely Orsorkon of Bubastis mentioned by Piye. (Psusennes was a Tanite king and Piye did not go that far north-east). The point however is that again we have close to corresponding dates, back to the time of Piye's invasion.

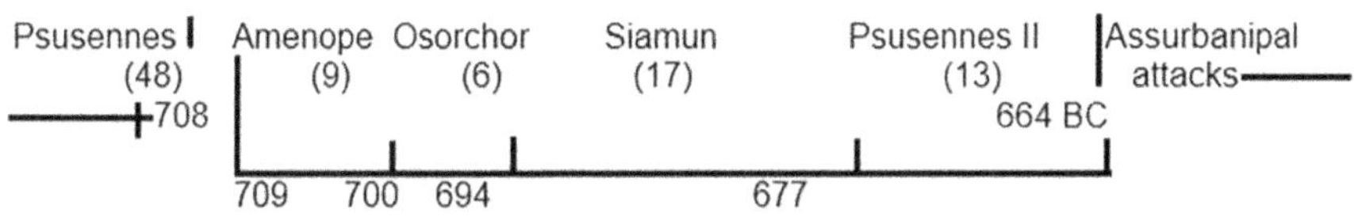

FOURTH - the 22nd Dynasty:-

Here we have some difficulties, but we start at the end with Pedubast II's 10 year reign - to 674 BC, almost certainly the 'Putubishti of Sa'nu' (Tanis), mentioned by Assurbanipal - ARAB 2, 771.

The son of Sheshonk V- 38 years (the latter year mentioned by Tefnakht II), who is believed to have been co-regent with Sheshonk III his grandfather for a period. This complicates the maths, and his father Pa'mai (Pimay) almost certainly reigned parallel with Sheshonk V, at Heracleopolis, not Tanis, but on the death of Sheshonk III, (so that Pimay's reign did not intervene between Sheshonk III and Sheshonk V). But we have already given reasons why the attack by Piye was around year 30 of Sheshonk III's reign-and dated that to 711 BC.

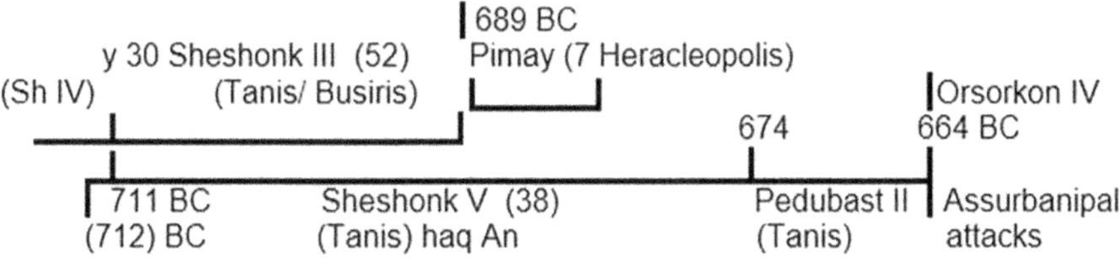

A close correlation appears as a result of the great chief of the Libu Niumateped who was contemporary with, year 13 Takelot II = year 10 of Sheshonk III (731 BC), and year 24 of Piye = year 33 of Sheshonk III (23 years), but not mentioned on the large Dakleh stele which most likely dates to the 5th year of Sheshonk VI = circa. year 33-34 Sheshonk III.

As mentioned earlier Serapeum Sheshonk V Stela of year 37 equates in time with Stela year 14 of Taharqa.

FIFTH - the 23rd Dynasty, of Thebes gives us no primary strong anchor points except for the previous relationships discussed. Montemhat A (also 4PA), following on the death of Takelot III, Montemhat A most likely came to power 2-3 years before Assurbanipal's attack, but exactness seems not possible.

However Orsorkon B came to power 39th year of Sheshonk III (here -703/2 BC), for 28 years, so to 673/4 BC, followed by Takelot III for 13 years which includes a 5 year co-regency, hence 8 years sole (but this 13 years is in doubt as indicated in my discussion of the Dakleh Stelae, and so only 7 years), followed by Montemhat A who was then in power officially as Mayor of Thebes at the time of Assurbanipal's attack 664 BC, but how many years?

The highest residual date of Takelot III then is year 7, but we do not know whether that is sole reign or has co-regency within it, (but most likely the latter - then 2 years sole).

Another possible variable is the person of Sheshonk VIa (Si-ese), a year 5 stated. But what we do know is that Montemhat A was in place in 664 BC.

The addition on the assumptions of 2 sole years only of Takelot III and followed by 5 years of Sheshonk VIa would then leave an approximate 2 year margin for Mentemhat A before 664 BC.

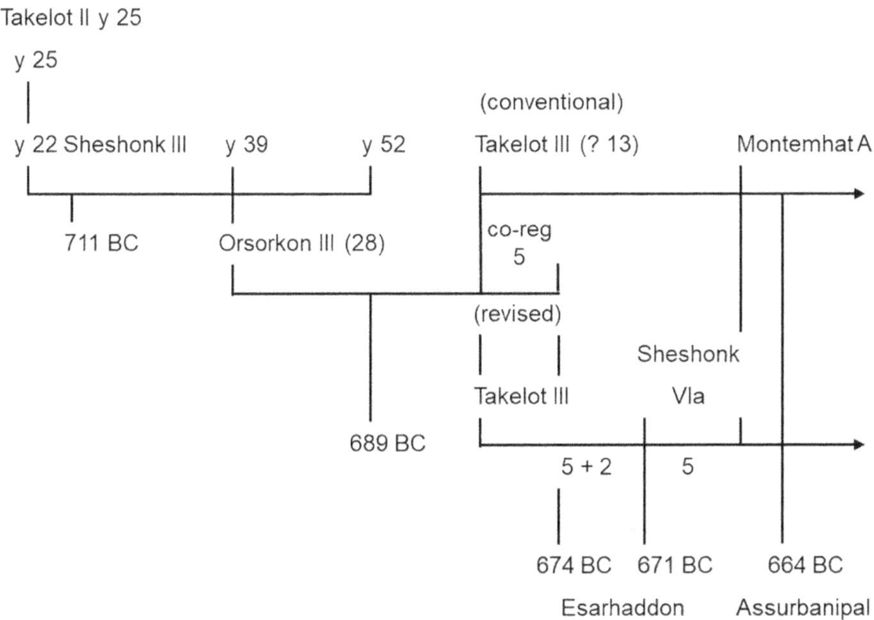

Kitchen p 350 places the 11th year of Orsorkon III equivalent to year 1 of Sheshonk V (Kitchen p. 350), and on the basis of the above graphs (4th and 5th sections)- a rough closeness of these two agrees with that, with 1st SOLE year of Sheshonk V circa.689 BC and 11th year of Orsorkon III circa. 691-690 BC, (but such calculation has not aimed for exactness).

SIXTH - the 20th Dynasty (and it's correlation with the early 22nd Dynasty):-

This Dynasty is not difficult to place overall, but is difficult to absolute date, but we have here close relationships with Ramses XI, Pinudjem I (*Kheperkhare*)- 21st Dyn., Smendes I (21st Dyn.)., as well as synchronisms with many of the priestly caste of Thebes, Memphis and Heracleopolis, the approximate dates for these kings are discussed above. This Dynasty had ended some years before Piye's attack, most likely by a decade.

Taking the dates back further is more difficult, but Smendes I's 15 year corresponds to the beginning of the reign of Pinudjem I *Kheperkhare* (who reigned 10 years, but almost certainly at advanced age). This date corresponds to the death of Ramses XI (his y 30 conventional, y 33 Thijs).

Now Smendes I *Nesubanebdjed* was son-in-law to Ramses XI, as was Pinudjem I *Kheperkhare.*

As discussed earlier there was significant overlap of Orsorkon II and Orsorkon I, and the suggestion is strong that Orsorkon I was significantly in parallel in reign with father Sheshonk I, especially while Takelot I was alive.

I have provisionally suggested that Sheshonk I began his tenure, then, around 770 BC, appointed in Heracleopolis \ Bubastis \ Tanis in some official capacity by Ramses II approximately after that king's 22nd year.

This then suggests that the 'third intermediate period' occupied 106 years only and ran parallel with the sequence:- 23rd year of the reign of Ramses II to Merenptah then to Dynasty 25 which was ended by Assurbanipal 664 BC.

Now correlation here purely using reign terms is singularly difficult, but if we use the most likely LIFE-TIMES, as opposed to just YEARS OF REIGN, then the above relationships are entirely credible.

To arrive at this several reasonable assumptions are necessary

1) An assumption that each king lived up to 20 years before any significant family (although evidence exists of children produced by some a few years earlier, even as early as their 14th year of life).
2) An assumption that Sheshonk I lived at least to his 70th year and so had a significant family by the time of his appointment 21 years before. (such would include Orsorkon I, and possibly Sheshonk's IIa *-Heqakheperre*, Sheshonk IIb - *Tutkheperre*,)
3) This would mean that son Orsorkon I was quite mature, and that he also likely had son Takelot I already out of that kings teen years, reigning for 14 years, and able to beget son Orsorkon II, who clearly came to the throne very young

The NEXUS of 20th and 22nd DYNASTIES -THE 'HAQ AN' FACTOR.

The 20th Dynasty was almost certainly centred at Heliopolis and a number of it's kings bore the title HAQ AN. Viz. Ramses III, Ramses VI, Ramses VII then Ramses XI.

I have previously argued that it is almost certain that Ramses VI and VII co-reigned at Heliopolis with the early years of Ramses III, and that the early years of Ramses XI were also a co-reign with the later years of Ramses III, - Ramses XI then in sole reign approximately another 25 years, giving a total reign of the 20th Dynasty between 50-54 years.

The next kings that held the title of HAQ AN were in order Sheshonk III, Sheshonk IV, Sheshonk V.

It appears Sheshonk III took the title and rule of Heliopolis sometime in the twenties of his reign, and I believe he would have taken the title from the now collapsed 20th Dynasty, possibly close to 718 BC (we certainly know that Sheshonk III had the title of ruler of Heliopolis by year 28 - Serapaeum stelae 22 and 24 - Beckerath 1999 p 188 -189 -Handbuch der Agyptisch Konigsnamen), and as above we place Sheshonk V's reign termination 674 BC.

An alternate moment would be the 19th year of Ramses XI when he moved his administration from Heliopolis to Thebes.

This would suggest that the 20th Dynasty came to power circ. sometime around or just after 767 BC (but possibly 763 for Ramses III, and as an approximation I have earlier equated the 8th year of Ramses III in his conflict with the Sea People circ. 755 BC - bearing in mind that exactness is unlikely here).

The above discussion then would suggest that the early 22nd Dynasty, of Tanis, Bubastis, and Heracleopolis Magna, up to the circa. 24th year of Sheshonk III were concurrent with the 20th Dynasty at Heliopolis, allowing around just over 50 years for that portion of the 22nd Dynasty, and such would involve a number of overlapping and parallel rules. (we are aware of details allowing parallelisms with Sheshonk I, Orsorkon I, Takelot I and early Orsorkon II, as well as parallelisms between Sheshonk III, Takelot II and some of the rule of Orsorkon II).

ARRANGEMENT of 22nd DYNASTY BEFORE THE INVASION OF PIYE

Petrie vol III, p. 247 mentions a monument (unpublished at that stage), indicating that Harsiese HPA (B) was 'associated' with Orsorkon II - the latter's 23rd year.

The following diagram then illustrates the result:-

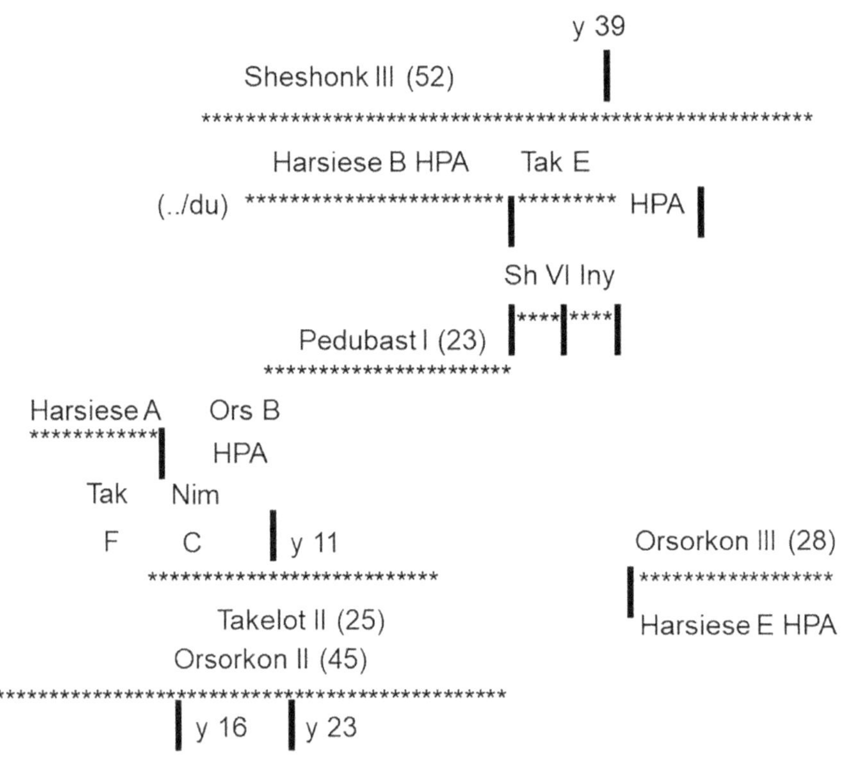

The 22nd Dynasty prior to Takelot II's accession is slightly less definable, but we have the evidence previously mentioned that there must have been a significant overlap of Orsorkon I and early Orsorkon II, as well as a significant parallel reign between Sheshonk I and son Orsorkon I, the reign of Takelot I almost certainly being parallel with Orsorkon I but before Orsorkon II. The result demands that the time period covered by these reigns, prior to the decease of Orsorkon I was less than 30 years and that a short period occurred with the sole rule of Orsorkon II, probably less than 10 years before Orsorkon II elevated Takelot II to the throne of Thebes in 747 BC.

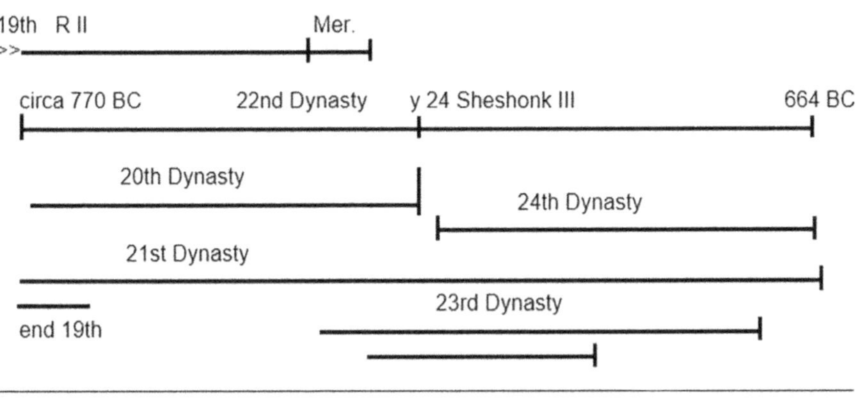

SOME OUTSTANDING QUESTIONS

There are two groups of evidence which form a stumbling-block to this revision. viz. Appendix - A) The statues listing the genealogy of the Neseramun family, and Appendix - B) the List of High Priests of Ptah of Memphis in the Berlin Stela and Louvre Stela.

APPENDIX A

THE NESERAMUN FAMILY

The details here are found in the Cairo Catalogues 42219 (C19), and 42220 - 4 (C 20, 21, 22, 23, 24), and read, with the conventional chronology in mind appear to confirm that chronology. Added to the information is Karnak Priestly Annal 3B which mentions the induction of certain people who appear related to that family.

The particular argument centres around the family line:-

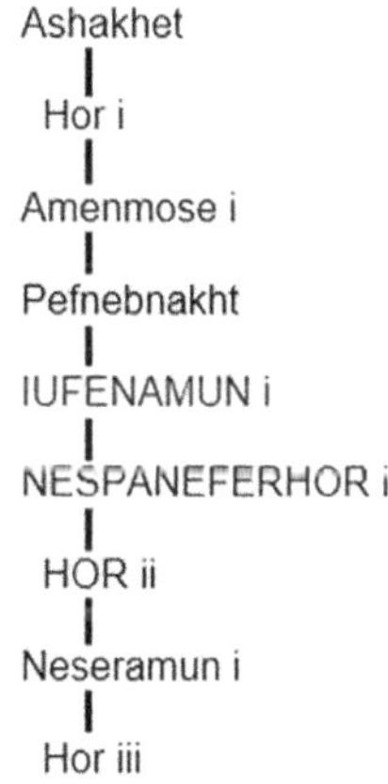

Hor iii can be identified married to Itawy ii, daughter of Djedthutefankh and Tashenbast daughter of Sheshonk I.

With that identification there seems to be no problem.

But with Karnak Priestly Annal 3B we are given the details of Nespanefenhor son of Iufenamun being inducted into priestly office year 2 of Akheperre (Osorchor), and his son Hor(i) into office year 17 of Siamun.

These are then assumed (not unreasonably-conventionally) to be the same personages as those found in the list of the family of Neseramun. But an assumption it is.

The burials at Tanis suggest that Dyn. 21 (containing Osorchor and Siamun) must have had a significant overlap with Dyn. 22 (Rohl), to such an extent that Osorchor and Siamun would have been to some extent contemporary with Sheshonk III and early Sheshonk V.

Evident at that period and in the genealogy of Neseramun is the quite frequent generational repetition of names, so that without absolute correlation of these people it is reasonable to suggest that another family Iufenamun-> Nespaneferhor -> Hor later existed, repeating the names of previous ancestors (possibly still within the Neseramun family en-clave).

Bierbrier mentions several Iufenamun's around that time (Chart XII p. 51, and p. 129 note 208), and Kitchen mentions at least 3 Nespaneferhor's, and No. ii-index, could well be the person mentioned here (Section 12 note 65), as well as a Iufenamun at a significantly appropriate time on this revised chronology (section 16 note 89).

I, therefore, suggest that Iufenamun of kitchen's chart (of 166), C 21 and 24, and Nespanefenhor of C 19-21 and 24, are NOT the same people as on Karnak 3B, and Hor of Karnak 3B and Theban tomb 68 of Nespaneferhor is NOT the same as Hor ii, but most likely are in a parallel line several generations later of the same family, repeating names of revered ancestors.

Priestly appointments of note:-

(Karnak Priestly Annals 3B lines 1-5)
Iufenamun
|
Block Karnak 94 CL2149
Osorchor y 2 → Nespaneferhor ? same Kitchen 12 n. 65, no. 98.
|
(Neseramun)
Nesamun Siamun y 17 → Hori
|
Nesankhefenmaat > y 11 Psusennes II (KPA 3B line 6 -year 13)
| (?4PA)
Hor → Y 3 Orsorkon (?IV)

APPENDIX B

CORRELATION AGAINST BERLIN STELE

Stele Berlin 23673 and LOUVRE '96'; Cat. 52.

These stelae, giving lists of High Priests of Ptah at Memphis have been assumed to agree with the conventional sequential dynastic arrangement, but on close inspection they in fact agree with the parallelisms presented in this revision. Two anomalies reveal themselves against an interpretation on a purely sequential manner:-

a) A break in the list between Ramses II (19th) and Amenemnisu (21st), without a break in genealogy.
b) A parallel list in Louvre of High Priests during 21st Dynasty and 22nd Dynasty.
c) An additional anomaly has revealed itself in an added list presented by El-Shakawy 2009, which appears to insert some extra High Priests.

Let us examine these:-

a) Kitchen 1986 p.189, states - "Thus for roughly 150 years or more from the death of Ramsses II to the early 21st Dynasty, the Berlin document

> has only *one* generation (Ptah-em-akhet B) between Ramesses II and Amenemnisu."

He then makes various suggestions to attempt an explanation, but one explanation he did not contemplate was parallelisms of dynasties.

The father of Ptah-em-akhet B was Neferronpet who was a vizier and High Priest of Ptah under Ramesses II (y 50, Kitchen 1982,chart II) but also Vizier (most likely at the same time) under Ramesses IV (Petrie), who I have earlier argued was early contemporary with his father Ramesses III, and mid to late Ramses II, (this correlation assumes the same person.Which would not fit with the conventional chronology but correlates closely on this revision).

Then Neferronpet's grandson Ashakhet 1 was contemporary with Amenemnisu, who was a son of Smendes I, the latter who in turn was married to Ramesses XI's daughter Tentamun B.

So, in this space El-Shakawy has presented 12 persons (not all related), many of whom were in office with kings of the 20th Dynasty (R III - R XI).

It is then clear that El-Shakawy's list is a list of officials parallel to the reign of Ramesses II. It is also of interest that Seti II is also mentioned contemporary with one of these - fitting my arrangement of the 'so-called' terminal 19th Dynasty, as a break-off, ruling in Thebes.

b) A parallel list presented in Louvre 96 of descendants of Ashakhet 1, but officials under Dynasty 22, while the Berlin list notes those under 21st Dynasty, both of these ending under Sheshonk V with an Ankhefensekhmet, and the possibility exists that these two latter were in fact one and the same, i.e a possible consort linking the families. But a clear contemporaneity of these two dynasties.

c) The Berlin list is assumed generally to be a genealogy, but there are problems in accepting that as complete, e.g. Ashakhet I (A in Kitchen), contemporary with Amenemnisu son of Smendes I is assumed to be the father of "Pipi I", but according to El Sharkawy this is not stated, and may in fact represent a break and a part parallelism.

The presence of Shedsunefertum being made a contemporary of Sheshonk I, would favour the conventional chronology, but the Sheshonk is '*Hedjkheperre sheshonk*', and Rohl has pointed clearly to another later *Hedjkheperre sheshonk* (now labelled IV, there now also being another now labelled Sheshonk VIa - *Siese meryamun*, and therefore likely associated with Thebes). Sheshonk IV may well be the son of Sheshonk III and had the title Haq An. If in fact the Sheshonk, supposed, contemporary with Shedsunefertum is the latter (which is eminently possible), then a confirmation with the shortened chronology here presented now exists. Kitchen mentions an embalming table made by Shedsunefertum with cartouches of "Sheshonk" (section 152, n. 7)

However, the relationship with a king 'Sheshonk I" is supposed on correlation with the conventional chronology and is not, in fact, demanded. Shedsunefentum is in fact said to have had a son Sheshonk HPM -(El Sharkawy -Louvre Stele).

Cairo cat. 741 :-

Ankhefensekhmet A = Tapeshenese (Tasherenese)

King x Great Chief (chief of harim of Ptah, priestess of Mut)

(c of P, p of M)

Mehteweshkhet = Shedsunefertum A (2 wives)

(c of P, p of M)

(daughter of great chief of the Ma)

Tentseper = "

(sister of the daughter of the lord of the two lands)

(or sister in law) (Kitchen p. 114)

(c of P, p of M)

(king's daughter) This is likely Kitchen's Tentseper B

Shedsunefertum contemporary with "great chief of Ma", Sheshonk III, but others also held that title at that period - ? at or before Piye. The above women's names were not uncommon from period Sheshonk I to Sheshonk III, the father-in-law, great chief of the Ma and King - lord of the two lands - (if the same), could be Sheshonk III, but another may be in mind, however the conventionally held Sheshonk I is chronologically out of contest, (see below)

If Shedsunefertum's wives were daughters of Sheshonk III, he would then be brother-in-law to Sheshonk IV *Hedjkheperre Sheshonk* as well as Pimay, which sits comfortably with his son Senebef (see below) being a priest and Seer of Ptah at time of king Pimay year 2, concurrent with Harsiese H (son of Pediese HPM) being HPM, allowing time between Pediese and Harsiese H for son of Shedsunefertum Sheshonk as HPM, then grandson Osorkon A HPM briefly followed by Takelot - sem priest.

Shedsunefertum may well have briefly held the HPM after Takelot B/C and before Pediese, if the above logic has merit.

Shedsunefentum HPM married a priestess of Mut,(El-Shakawy 2009) and either Mehtweshkhet or Tentseper would therefore both be candidates, however as kitchen points out this title could be the result of the marriage, as Shedsunefertum's mother held the title.

The "memorial Stone of the priest and Seer of Apis Bull of Senebef son of Shedsunefertum" is dated to the 2nd year of Pamai, therefore after the death of Sheshonk III. This then places Shedsunefertum well after Sheshonk I, allowing that the *Hedjkheperre Sheshonk* with whom he was contemporary was therefore likely Sheshonk IV likely son of Sheshonk III. However, that does not clarify the chronology of the reign of those latter two kings, whom I have previously suggested were parallel, not successive.

Another anomaly pointed out by Rohl is the fact that Stele Berlin has Amenemnisu before Psusennes, whereas Manetho has him after. But as Amenemnisu is believed to have reigned in parallel to Psusennes I, the authors then are left with a quandry as to whether they place him before or after in any linear sequence, so I do not see this as an anomaly.

Most scholars have assumed the interpretation against the conventional chronology and therefore made suggestions as to who were the contemporary kings, but the only certainties stated between Ashakhet I and Ankhefensekhmet, are Amenemnisu and Psusennes I, as well as Pipi B associated with Siamun (Kitchen p. 189), all the others are assumed on conventional grounds. And it should be added that the exact time relationship between Amenemnisu and Psusennes I is not settled.

d) The Louvre list with alternate names beginning Sheshonk C (or I), we most likely have here a confusion of labels, for El-Sharkawy points out that this Sheshonk (1) is in fact son of Shedsunefertum (No. 84 on his list), and the next on the list Orsorkon A (No. 85) is his son.

But the following one Sheshonk D (Louvre List) is in fact the son of king Orsorkon II, and the next 4, linear descendants of Sheshonk III son of Orsorkon II, as is also possible for the last Ankhefensekhmet. This indicates that Orsorkon II had now imposed a High Priestly line in parallel to the official family line, but this would have happened prior to the HPM of Shedsunenefertum, if the chronology above has merit.

El-Sharkawy then points out that Shedsunefertum had 5 sons and 2 daughters.

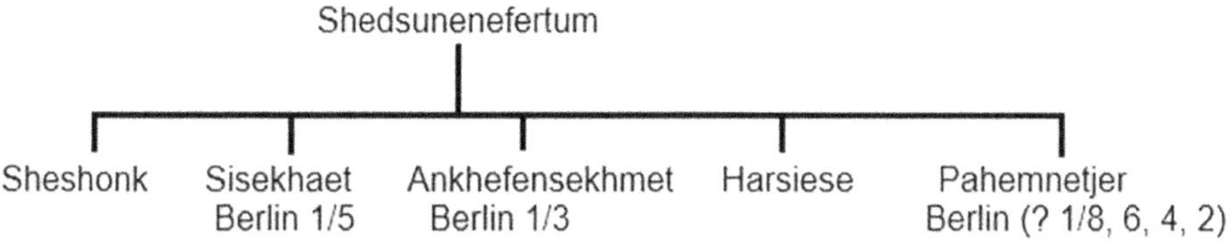

The Memorial Stone of the priest and Seer of Apis Bull Senebef also adds two more sons - Senebef and Hor-heb, both priests.

Rohl (1996 p. 56) states with regard to the Apis Stelae (the representatives for Ptah of Memphis):-

> *"One so far inexplicable aspect of the finds from the Serapeum is the complete lack of stelae for the whole 21st Dynasty and for the first half of the 22nd Dynasty.—"*

It would be natural to feel that this is simply failure to have so far found them, but when the 22nd Dynasty is examined, involvement with Ptah of Memphis first begins with Orsorkon II, four generations into the dynasty with Apis recorded for Orsorkon II, Takelot II, Sheshonk III and descendants with mention of 4 later generations. And the Louvre records of High Priest of Ptah from this line begins with a son of Orsorkon II - Sheshonk D, with the exception of the sons of Shedsunefertum.

The Berlin list corresponding concerns a long priestly family and they are related in time to kings of the 21st Dynasty of northern Tanis. -Amenemnisu to Siamun, none of whom appear to have record of association with Apis Stelae.

The correspondence then may not be accidental but real, in view of Rohl's discussion of dynasty parallelism, the 22nd more temporal dynasty having dominance with the record of the Memphis priesthood and some kind of dual arrangement being practiced.

In view of the earlier discussion which places Shedsunefertum contemporary with and brother-in-law to Takelot B/C HPM, Sheshonk IV *Hedjkheperre sheshonk* and Pimay, and the suggestion that his wives are the daughters of "great chief of the Ma, the lord of the two lands" Sheshonk III, this places Shedsunefertum right into the family relationship of Sheshonk' III.

With that we can perhaps arrange the alternate HPMs in following order:-

Sheshonk D	son of Orsorkon II	
Merenptah	? Is this in fact Merenptah son of Ramses II ?	
Takelot B/C	son of Sheshonk III	
Shedsunefertum	son in-law to Sheshonk III	
Pediese	son of Takelot B/C	
Peftjauawybast	son of Pediese	
Sheshonk C	son of Shedsunefertum	priest Senebef son of Shedsunefertum
Orsorkon A	son of the Sheshonk C	sem priest Takelot A son of Sheshonk C
Harsiese H	son of Pediese	cont. Pimay
Ankhefensekhmet	son of Harsiese H (or ? son of Shedsunefertum) cont Sheshonk V	

HPMs from priestly line, are related on records to 21st Dynasty, but it should be noted that the 21st Dynasty was intimately related to the late 20th Dynasty

Berlin	1/15	Ashakhet I	Amenemnisu
"	1/14	Pipi I	Psusennes I
"	1/13	Horsiese J	Psusennes I
"	1/12	Pipi B	Psusennes (to Siamun)
"	1/11	Ashakhet II	

We then would have an arrangement similar to the following:- DYN. 22

Berlin 2/2 Neferronpet	Ramses II		
" 2/1 Ptahemakhet			
" 1/15 Ashakhet I	Amenemnisu		
" 1/14 Pipi I	Psusennes I — Louvre Sheshonk D ORS II		
" 1/13 Horsiese J	Psusennes I	Louvre Merenptah	
" 1/12 Pipi B	Psusennes I to Siamun	Louvre Takelot (B) Sh III	
" 1/11 Ashakhet II			

possible gap here assumed in priestly genealogy record, with no guarantee of family relationship.

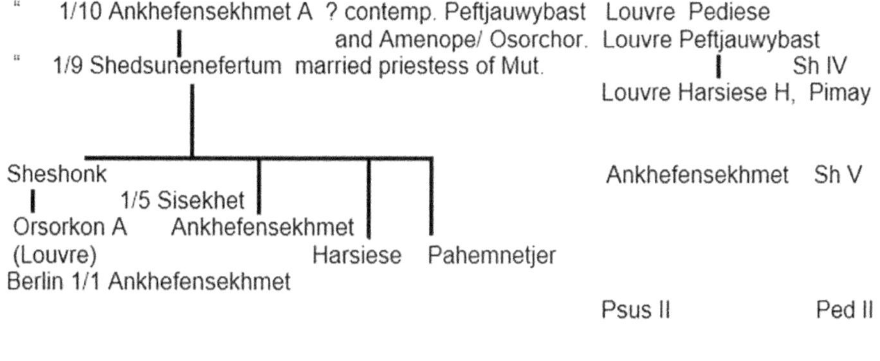

e) David Rohl's strong and logical argument that Orsorkon II (22nd Dyn.), must have been buried before Psusennes I (21st Dyn.) should also mitigate against interpretation of these lists against the conventional chronology.

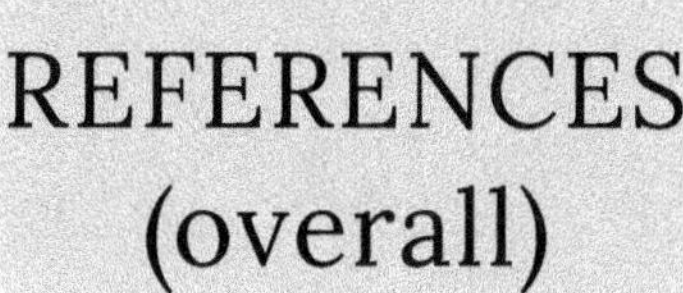

REFERENCES (overall)

Aston JEA 75, 1989, “Takeloth II - A King of the ‘Theban Twenty-Third Dynasty’, p139-153.

ARAB vol. II, Luckenbill, Daniel David, 1927, Ancient Records of Assyria and Babylonia vol II, Greenwood Press New York.

Beckerath , Jurgen von, 1999, Handbuch der Agyptisch Konigsnamen, p. 188-189,

Bierbrier, M.L.,1975, “The Late New Kingdom of Egypt”. Aris and Phillips Ltd. Warminster.

Blackman, JEA 27, 1941, p 83-95.

Courville, Donovan. The Exodus Problem and its Ramification.

De Puydt, Leo, 1993, JEA 79, p. 269

Dodson and Hilton, 2004, The Complete Royal families of Ancient Egypt, Thames and Hudson, London

Dothan. M. 1972, Ashdod - Seven Seasons of Excavation, Qadmoiot 5:2-13 (Hebrew)
1981a Notes and News, ‘Akko. IEJ 31:110-112.
1982b, The Beginning and End of Archaeological periods at Adjacent Sites. EI 15:151-153 (Hebrew)

Dothan T. 1982b. What We Know about the Philistines. Biblical Archaeological review 8:20-44.

El-Sharkawy, Dr. Basem, 2009, A New List of the High Priests of Ptah at Memphis (PART 2), Abgadiyat 4 (Alexandria 2009) p. 69-85.

Finkelstein, Israel 1995, Tel Aviv vol. 22 / 2, p 213-239.

Gardiner Sir Alan, 1933, JEA 19.

Green, Alberto R.W. 1993, April, JNES 52, No. 2, 'The Identity of King So of Egypt'

Herodotus, The Hiistories, Book 2, p. 154, 124. Penguin Classics.

Jacquet-Gordon, Helen K. 1960, The Philadelphia Statue of Orsorkon II. p12-23.

James Peter 2013. Two Studies in 21st Dynasty History 1: Deconstructing Manetho's 21st Dynasty II: The dateline of High Priest Menkheperre.
Journal of Egyptian History 6:1 219-256.

Jansen-Winkein Karl 1992, "Das Ende des Neuen Reiches", Zeitschrift fur Agyptische Sprache, 119 p 22-37.

Janssen Jac J. 1968 JEA 54.

Kahn, Dan'el, The Libyan period in Egypt,Historical and Cultural Studies into the 21st-24th Dynasties: Proceedings of a conference at Leiden University 25-27, 2007, pp.139-148.

Kitchen, K.A, 'Pharaoh Triumphant' The Life and Times of Ramesses II,1982, Aris and Phillips Ltd. Warminster.

Kitchen, K.A. The third Intermediate Period in Egypt, second edition 1986 Aris & Phillips Ltd, p 339-40.

Luckenbill, Daniel David, Ancient Records of Assyria and Babylonia (ARAB), Vol. 1 and 2. (Greenwood Press New York)

Lulli Jose 2009, Beginning and End of High Priest of Amun Menkheperre. The Libyan period in Egypt. Historical and Cultural Studies into 21st -24th Dynasties. Proceedings of a conference at Leiden University 25-27 October 2007.

Manley, Bill 1996 The Penguin Historical Atlas of Ancient Egypt.

Montet, Pierre, 1928, Byblos et l'Egypte, Quatre Campagnes des Fouilles 1921-1924 p 226-238, Paris. reprint Beirut 1998.

Niwinski, Andrzej, 1979, JARCE, vol. XVI, p 51& 60.

Perdu, Oliver 2002, Comptes rendus des seances de l'academi des Inscriptions et Belles-Lettres 146 (4) 1215-1244.

Petrie, Sir Flinders, History of Egypt, p 71. History of Egypt vol III p 174-175, Koptos Stele (P. Kop XIX)

Rohl, David, A Test of Time, 1995, Century Publications.

Shea, William H. 1985, Journal of Biblical literature Vol.104 No. 3, p 401-418.

Singer, Itamar, 1985 Tel Aviv 12 / 2, p 109-122.

Suriano, Matthew J. Biblical Odyssey, "The Samaria Ostraca"

Tallet,P, Bickel, S, & Gaboide, M, 1998,"Des annales heliopolitanes de la Troisieme Periode Intermediane" BIFO 98: 31-56.

Taylor John H.T. 1995, Proceedings of the seventh International Congress of Egyptologists 3-9th September. p.1148.

Thijs Ad 2011, Introducing the Banishment Stele into the 20th Dynasty, Zeitschrift fur Agyptische Sprache und Altertum vol 138, p169.

Weggalaar, Nel, and Kort Chris, University of Amsterdam, "The Calendar Reforms of Ancient Egypt"- no date given.

www.ingramcontent.com/pod-product-compliance
Lightning Source LLC
LaVergne TN
LVHW020627100826
845148LV00012B/2088

* 9 7 8 1 7 6 4 4 4 3 0 8 1 *